Program Notes
for the
Solo Tuba

COMPILED AND EDITED BY
Gary Bird

INDIANA UNIVERSITY PRESS
Bloomington and Indianapolis

© 1994 by Indiana University Press
All rights reserved

The paper used in this publication meets the minimum requirements of
American National Standard for Information Sciences—Permanence of
Paper for Printed Library Materials, ANSI Z39.48–1984.
∞ ™

Manufactured in the United States of America

Library of Congress Cataloging-in-Publication Data

Program notes for the solo tuba / compiled and edited by Gary Bird.
    p.   cm.
    ISBN 0–253–31189–6
    1. Tuba music—History and criticism.   I. Bird, Gary.
ML973.P76   1994
788.9'8—dc20   93–34073

1 2 3 4 5 99 98 97 96 95 94

Contents

PART TWO: **Composer Profiles**

Foreword

Harvey Phillips
Distinguished Professor of Music, Indiana University, Bloomington

With this collection of program notes, almost all of them by the composers, Gary Bird has provided both tubists and public audiences with important information about solo compositions for the tuba. These notes will inspire tubists to more definitive interpretations and give audiences a better understanding and enjoyment of the music performed. Composers who have not yet written solo works for tuba, on studying the descriptive accounts, especially those written by the composers themselves, may be inspired to do so.

Far too often I have heard composers, on reading program notes describing their works, ponder, "Who wrote these notes?" "Where did they get this?" "That's not my piece they're writing about!" "They didn't analyze my composition, they annihilated it!" Several times I encouraged my doctoral students, including Gary Bird, to propose the compilation of program notes for their dissertation, but each time the proposal was declined. Fortunately, for all of us who play the tuba and/or compose for it, Gary Bird chose to initiate and pursue the project. His excellent research will ensure the success of this book and, I hope prompt future publications of a similar nature.

June 1993

Preface

Part One of *Program Notes for the Solo Tuba* consists of 88 articles describing some of the most important compositions written for solo tuba. Each note was written by the composer of the work or by someone who has studied the compositions and styles of the composer. It lists the complete title, publisher and date, number and names of the movements, and instrumentation. It also recounts any interesting circumstances surrounding the conception of the work (a commission, a contest piece, a special occasion, *Gebrauchsmusik*, etc.) and comments on its structure, its musical characteristics, and sometimes its recording history.

This compilation includes works for tuba alone and tuba with a variety of accompanying ensembles: with piano, woodwind quintet, string quartet, band, orchestra, etc. References to pitch range in the tuba parts are based on the following scheme, in which middle C of the piano keyboard is designated as c (one line above the bass staff). The octave ascending from middle C is written: c, d, e, f, g, a, b, c¹.

c^2 c^1 C   c   c c^1 c^2 c^3

Part Two profiles five deceased composers who were among the most important and influential to have written solos for the tuba: Paul Hindemith, Vincent Persichetti, Halsey Stevens, Ralph Vaughan Williams, and Alec Wilder. Their biographies, written by scholars who were close to the composers and/or their music, offer insights into the composers' overall output as well as their impact on the totality of twentieth-century music.

It is hoped that *Program Notes for the Solo Tuba* will serve as a convenient reference for students, teachers, and performers, both professional and amateur.

PART ONE

The Repertoire

Samuel Adler (b. 1928)

Samuel Adler is Professor of Composition and Chair of the Composition Department at the Eastman School of Music, University of Rochester, Rochester, NY.

Canto VII for Solo Tuba

New York: Boosey and Hawkes, 1974.
Movements: I. Quite fast
              II. Light, fluffy, and quick
              III. Slowly and with great expression
              IV. Fast and triumphant
Instrumentation: Tuba Alone

Canto VII was written in October 1972 at the suggestion of Harvey Phillips and is dedicated to him. It is the seventh in a series of solo pieces beginning with a four-movement work for trumpet and including concert etudes for trombone, violin, saxophone, an ensemble consisting of voice, flute, cello, and two percussion players, double bass, tuba, piano, timpani, cello, and horn, in that order.

In each of the Cantos I have tried to feature as much of the possibilities of each instrument as necessary to create a solo work which would stand up in a concert performance, challenge the performer, and present each instrument in as many roles and colors as feasible. Each of the instruments suggested certain form, and therefore no Canto is necessarily related to any other. Looking back on the series now, I find a slight relationship between the ones for trumpet, trombone, and tuba, since these are the only ones written in four movements; that is as far as the similarities go.

Canto VII begins with a series of low Fs, which are to be "punched out" as heavily as possible. These melt into a long held F and lead into a rather lyrical first movement based on the minor second, major and minor third, and perfect fourth.

Much of the pitch material is derived from these intervals, although their inversions as well as other intervals do occur for contrast and relief, with the tritone acting as a pivotal and cadence point.

The second movement is a theatre piece. It is my hope that the tubist as well as the audience will have a good time with valve clicks, fingernails tapping on the instrument, air being forced through the tubes without pitches, and foot stamping. It should be a scherzo-romp executed as rhythmically, quickly, and comically as possible.

The third movement should demonstrate the immense power and the expressiveness of the tuba. It is a "sound piece" and should be used to amplify the beauty of the instrument with delicate lines and very powerful moments of *crescendi* to maximum sound. One must be sure to plan gradations of softness and loudness so that the entire gamut of dynamics can be demonstrated.

The final movement is a variant of the first. It contains many of the gestures of the opening movement with variations, to bring this short work to a logical musical conclusion. Care should be taken to pace the first and fourth movements so that the relationship of the two is evident.

Eugene D. Anderson (b. 1944)

Eugene D. Anderson is a former tuba instructor at Arizona State University. He is the founder of Anderson's Arizona Originals.

Concert Piece for Tuba and Band

Apache Junction, AZ: Anderson's Arizona Originals, 1984.
Movements: One Movement—Fast, Slow, Fast
Instrumentation: Tuba and Band

This work was written in the summer of 1984 for a premier with the composer as soloist with the Mesa City (Arizona) Band, directed by Tom Kacere. It is intended to feature the tuba in a challenging work, with the band as an equal partner. The range of the tuba is three octaves, and the solo part requires double tonguing.

The *Concert Piece* has three completely different contrasting themes and has a format of fast, slow, fast. In the first fast section the first theme is presented alone, alternately by soloist and band, as it is partially developed. The slow section features the second theme with tuba, trombone, and baritone sections with the soloist, then the full band. The piece is then slowed by several fermatas and modulates from B♭ minor to C major. The third theme now enters; it is lyrical and singing, played by woodwinds and solo tuba. Clarinets take the theme as the tuba plays a counter-melody to close this section.

The sudden allegro announces the final section, as all three themes are further developed and finally used in counterpoint. The rousing coda closes the *Concert Piece* in a convincing and satisfying way.

This piece should please musicians and audiences alike. The music is challenging to play yet fun and enjoyable to listen to. It should be easy to program successfully with a good high school band or better. The total length of the work is 5′ 30″. The solo tuba has a range of three octaves, F^1 to f, and requires fast technique for the allegro sections, a lyrical singing style up to high F in the slow section, and double tonguing near the end.

Concerto No. 1 in B minor for Tuba and Orchestra

Apache Junction, AZ: Anderson's Arizona Originals, 1970.
Movements: I. Legato espressivo
              II. Largo
            III. Allegro
Instrumentation: Tuba and Orchestra

This major work, composed between 1968 and 1971, was written for Arnold Jacobs and the great Chicago Symphony. At 36

minutes in length, it is probably the longest solo work ever
written for the tuba, or perhaps for any brass instrument. Each
movement can be played alone, but the full impact is felt only
when all three are played in their entirety, since they are
linked thematically.

The two main reasons for composing this work were to
create a great piece of solo literature for the tuba, and to fill
the void of the period 1810–1900, when the tuba played in the
orchestra yet no composer ever wrote a concerto for it. This
work has accomplished both objectives and has added some
unique twentieth-century effects.

The first movement, in sonata allegro form, has four related
themes—A, B, C, and D—not the usual two. They are developed in counterpoint until three of them appear together at
the climax at bar 243. Even though the movement has some
big climactic points, it ends quietly, with a variation on the
introduction, since we are a long way from finished.

This leads effectively into the second movement, which is
based on a single theme, a Swedish lullaby, which the composer learned from his immigrant grandparents. The theme is
introduced hauntingly by the English horn. It then is reworked
in fifteen variations. The program underlying the variations
depicts a child being sung to sleep. As sleep deepens the child
dreams many dreams (variations). Finally one of the dreams
turns into a nightmare, with the now-grotesque theme filled
with meter changes. The child wakes in fright, and the music
stops. Then the music of the lullaby and its retrograde, played
simultaneously, lull the child to sleep once again and the
movement fades into nothingness.

The driving pace of the last movement, a rondo, bursts upon
the scene with a fury. The first theme (A) is dramatic, full of
excitement and color. The richly harmonized romantic second
theme (B) contrasts with the first as much as possible. The
later return of A and B is richly varied and even uses a percussion section in a four-part fugetta. But, now comes a twist: a
coda—not to the third movement but a coda for all three
movements, like none before it in music history.

We hear the main themes of each of the three movements
alone at first, then in pairs in counterpoint. Finally, as the

coda builds to the main climactic point at bar 281, the main themes of all three movements plus the accompaniment and counter-melody of the third movement theme all appear simultaneously, bringing this large work to an exciting close.

The playing requirements for the solo instrument are double and triple tonguing, a range from pedal C^2 to high g#, and tremendous endurance and technique, especially for the fast third movement. A large horn is preferred in order to compete with a full orchestra, usually a CC tuba.

Theodore Antoniou (b. 1935)

Theodore Antoniou, Professor of Music at Boston University, Boston, MA, is also a conductor.

Six Likes for Tuba, Op. 33

Kassel: Bärenreiter Verlag, 1967.
Movements: I. Like a Duet
                   II. Like a Study
                  III. Like a March
                  IV. Like a Cackling
                   V. Like a Song
                  VI. Like a Murmuring
Instrumentation: Tuba alone

Antoniou is essentially a dramatic composer. This does not imply that his compositions are always combined with some text. Characteristically, the composer himself refers to his work as "abstract program music," where "program" may denote an abstract, a musical, or an extramusical idea (e.g., space, instrumental techniques, etc.). Although Antoniou sometimes uses serial techniques, he does so in an original and personal way by recasting the methods to meet the specific demands of the piece.

His interest in developing a work lies in the musical possibilities of his material, rather than in its formalistic aspects.

Many of his works have a neo-folkloristic character. However, in the organization of the sound material, he makes use of new, sometimes avant-garde ways of expression (new compositional conceptions, instrumental and vocal techniques, performance practices, etc.). Through these techniques, together with his imaginative sense of the sound possibilities, he achieves an original expression in terms of sound structure and virtuosity.

In order to cope with the complex sound structures found in his works, he has developed a very flexible and innovative notation. In the full score, he makes use of a synthetic notation which describes, in an abbreviated way, all the necessary information on the sound structure. This enables the description of clusters, the movement of cluster, sound blocks, etc., to be notated in a visually efficient way for the conductor.

His *Six Likes, Op. 33*, was written in 1967 for the Second Hellenic Week, composed especially for the tubist Y. Zouganellis. It is based on the soloist's virtuoso potentialities, reaching to the extreme possibilities of the instrument. The movements are written in free forms, each one being developed on the basis of a special feature; the two middle movements are in the nature of parodies.

Jan Bach (b. 1937)

Jan Morris Bach is Professor of Music and University Research Professor of Theory and Composition at Northern Illinois University, DeKalb, IL.

Quintet for Tuba and Strings

Annandale, VA: T.U.B.A. Manuscript Press, 1986.
Movements: I. Introit (Tranquillo)
             II. Scherzo in moto perpetuo
                 (Fast but effortlessly)
            III. Chacone (Inquieto)
             IV. Ripresa e Fandango (Pesante)
Instrumentation: Tuba and String Quartet

Quintet for Tuba and Strings was written in the late summer of
1978 at the request of Harvey Phillips. Its composition was supported in part by a grant from the Northern Illinois University
Graduate School. The premiere was given by Harvey Phillips
and a string quartet of Indiana University graduate students on
January 6, 1980, at New York's Carnegie Recital Hall.

The opening movement, "Introit," is a dialogue which alternates between an insistent motto played by the quartet and
quiet, answering comments by the solo brass instrument. It is
cast in a broad arch shape in its dynamics, its range, the dura-
tions of its rhythms, and the densities of both its voices and its
timbres. This movement introduces most of the melodic and
harmonic material to be utilized in the ensuing movements.

The "Scherzo in moto perpetuo" is a simple ternary form
featuring many brilliant string effects against the more
straightforward tuba solos. In its outer sections, the strings
furnish a background of interlocking thirds in tremolo and
many special effects in short solos—harmonics, pizzicato, *sul
tasto, sul ponticello*, etc.—while the tuba apostrophizes each
solo string's statement. The quieter middle section features a
friendly game of one-upmanship in which the tuba attempts
in vain to stay even with the first violin.

The "Chaconne" is a set of variations on a harmonic progression which originally appeared as the climactic (i.e., middle)
section of the first movement. Its form, in the manner of the
"Introit," is an arch shape in its density, range, and rhythm.

The concluding "Ripresa e Fandango" begins with a re-
currence of the "Introit's" slow opening motto, now *pesante*
and divided between the unison strings and the tuba. This

motto functions as an introduction, becoming more and more agitated until it erupts into the faster body of the movement. Various ostinati, special effects, and rapid changes of mood and tempo abound in this section. Its drive toward the final double bar is interrupted only by a momentary musical hiatus in which the tuba's first-movement theme is recalled briefly.

David Baker (b. 1932)

David Baker is Distinguished Professor of Music specializing in Jazz Studies at Indiana University, Bloomington.

Piece for Solo Tuba and Tuba Quartet

Bloomington, IN: David Baker, 1990.
Movements: I. Haunting but with drive
               II. Slow and tenderly
               III. Fast with strong rhythm
Instrumentation: Solo Tuba and Tuba/Euphonium Quartet

Piece for Solo Tuba and Tuba Quartet is the result of a commission for a substantial work for virtuoso tubist Harvey Phillips and an exceptional tuba quartet consisting of Mary Ann Craig (first euphonium), Jay Hildebrandt (second euphonium), Gary Bird (F tuba), and Gregory Fritz (E♭ tuba). The technical demands made on the performers are, needless to say, conditioned by my knowledge of the abilities of these super players.

The work is between twelve and fifteen minutes in length. Movement I is virtuosic and lyrical, and is in sonata allegro form. The materials are basically modal. The solo tuba and the quartet are virtually equal in the demands made on them.

Movement II is slow, lyrical, and somewhat introspective. The solo tuba is placed very much in the spotlight and is allowed to sing freely.

Movement III is strongly rooted in jazz and uses character-istic scales, gestures, inflections, quasi-improvisational writing, and, above all, the pervasive feeling of the blues. As with move-ments I and II, the technical and expressive demands made on the performers are considerable. All other considerations aside, this work is intended as a fun piece.

Sonata for Tuba and String Quartet

Bloomington, IN: Frangipani Press, 1971.
Movements: I. Slow—Moderato
                 II. Easy swing "Blues"
                III. Very Slow
                IV. Fast
Instrumentation: Tuba and String Quartet

The *Sonata for Tuba and String Quartet*, written in 1971, is a work composed for and dedicated to my dear friend and col-league Harvey Phillips. Harvey and I had met earlier when we both played on a record date (*The Golden Striker*) for John Lewis on Atlantic Records. I had long admired his playing and healthy attitude vis-à-vis music in its totality. When we met again at a get-together of New England administrators, faculty, students, and alumni in Chicago during an MENC conven-tion, our minds were instantly of a single accord—a tuba piece, which would grow out of our rich and similar/dissimilar backgrounds.

The piece was over a year in unfolding but the result was this work, written for, at first glance, the unlikely combina-tion of tuba and string quartet. The choice of string quartet as the companion (not accompanying) group was very deliberate, and calculated to place the tuba in surroundings unlike those in which it usually finds itself. Because of Harvey's great artistry and sensitivity as well as the vast tonal combinatorial possibilities inherent in this unusual alliance, the string quar-tet provided the perfect foil.

The composition is in four movements, each designed to explore a different aspect of the quartet/tuba combination. The first and fourth are fast and in a loose sonata allegro form. Movement II is monothematic and draws very heavily in mood, harmonic structure, and note choice on the "blues." Movement III is slow and lyrical and combines elements of song form and sonata allegro. All four movements make extensive use of ostinato, virtuosic writing for tuba and strings, and intense rhythmic activity and drama. Three of the four movements open and close with the same material.

Movement I—Sonata Allegro Form
  1. Multi-layered rhythmic scheme.
  2. Extensive use of imitation.
  3. Multiple stopping.
  4. Fragmentation.
Movement II—Monothematic.
  1. "21st-century" blues introduced by solo tuba.
  2. Use of quarter tones in the repeat of theme.
  3. Principal technique is one of fragmentation.
  4. Humor.
Movement III—Sonata Form.
  1. Slow and lyrical.
  2. Use of strettos.
  3. Use of slides, slurs, and sudden changes in volume, mood, rhythms.
Movement IV—Sonata Allegro Form.
  1. Very fast.
  2. Opens with a virtuosic string passage in stretto and *sul ponticello*, over which the tuba soars with the (A) material.
  3. An ostinato combines with a tuba line for the (B) theme.
  4. A short cello and tuba duet, in which both instruments engage in double stops (for brass instruments this very difficult and modern technique is called multiphonics).
  5. A return to the virtuosic string opening leads to a strongly rhythmic coda culminating in a brilliantly executed ascending tuba line ending on a pedal C.

Bennie Beach (b. 1925)

Bennie Beach is Professor of Theory and Composition at Western Kentucky University, Bowling Green, KY.

Divertissement for Tuba

Bryn Mawr, PA: Theodore Presser Co., 1975.
Movements: I. Statement
             II. Waltz
             III. Chant
Instrumentation: Tuba alone

Divertissement for Tuba was written in the spring of 1974 as a studio study piece and is primarily designed to explore problems inherent in pitch definition and flexibility. More often than not, solutions to these problems are laborious and dull. In the Divertissement, I have endeavored to alleviate some of the drudgery in this kind of practice, by couching some of these technical problems in a musical setting. As a means to this end, I chose to use the twelve-tone method in the first two movements, believing that there is no better way to be on your own (or at sea) than to be with adjunct atonal material for three minutes, the lengths of movements I and II. For compositional balance and stylistic relief, the third movement is tonal (minor) and also three minutes in length. Flexibility and pitch definition continue to be targeted, and for a little added garnish, the middle section incorporates compound meters in a bright tempo.

The piece proved itself as a studio tool, both technically and musically. Satisfied with this, I released it and it was accepted for publication in 1975.

Movement I—Statement (free form).
1. Dramatic attitude is imperative.
2. Robust tone quality needed at all dynamic levels.
3. Disjunct intervals abound.
4. Unified rhythmic motif throughout.

Movement II—Waltz (modified ABA).
  1. Attitude must change with lighter approach to sound.
  2. Flowing, dancelike lines.
  3. A few disjunct intervals.
  4. Some extension and contraction.
Movement III—Chant (modified ABA).
  1. Feeling of incantation, as though notes are words.
  2. Dorian mode (B♭) at beginning resolving to (F) pure minor.
  3. Numerous meter changes throughout.
  4. Compound times and very bright tempo in section B. A
  quick change of mood is necessary here.
  5. Original mood returns and the piece ends quietly.

Rule Beasley (b. 1931)

Rule Beasley is Professor of Music at Santa Monica College,
Santa Monica, CA.

Concerto for Tuba and Band

Santa Monica, CA: Rule Beasley, 1968.
Movements: I. Allegro moderato
              II. Adagio—Allegro—Adagio
             III. Allegro vivace
Instrumentation: Tuba and Band

This composition was commissioned by my dear friend and colleague David Kuehn in 1968 and was given its first performance
at the University of North Texas with Dave as soloist. It is a
rather large-scale work of seventeen to twenty minutes actual
playing time. Each movement stands reasonably well alone,
and over the years, various public performances have featured
only one or the other of the three movements with satisfactory
results.

The composition style might be rather glibly described as "mid-twentieth-century conservative." The forms are conventional, and the notes are all written down on staff paper with traditional meter signatures, bar lines, rests, slurs, and dynamics. There are modal episodes, chord-building techniques from a wide variety of twentieth-century resources, avoidance of the "familiar concords" (triads), and a tendency to focus at strategic places on a central pitch as the tonal center of the section. This work does not include such devices as aleatory, steady-state effects, serialized ingredients, or atonality. Stylistically it lies somewhere between a Vaughan Williams and a Pierre Boulez.

As is to be expected from any concerto, the solo part is written to display the virtuosity of the soloist. There are long, lyric, expressive lines as well as rapid passage-work requiring a good brand of valve oil and an agile double-tonguing technique. The range is from F^1 to f.

Movement I: Allegro moderato, dotted quarter = 69, 6/8.

Flowing lines for the most part. The mood is gentle, reflective.

Movement II: Three sections (slow—fast—slow).

Adagio, quarter note = 76, 4/4.

Allegro, quarter note = 132, 2/4.

Adagio, quarter note = 76, 4/4.

This is a typical ABA plan with a scherzo-like middle part surrounded by slow and sedate moods.

Movement III: Allegro vivace, quarter note = 126–132, 3/4.

This largest and most rhythmically intense of the three movements ends with a virtuoso flourish.

Thomas Beversdorf (1924–1981)

Thomas Beversdorf studied with Kent Kennan at the University of Texas, Bernard Rogers and Howard Hanson at the Eastman School, and Aaron Copland and Darius Milhaud at the Berkshire Music Center. He taught at the University of Houston and was first trombonist with the Houston Symphony Orchestra, 1946–48; and from 1949 until his death, he was Professor of Music at Indiana University. His compositions include works for the stage, chorus, orchestra, and chamber ensemble as well as solo sonatas and concertos.

Sonata for Bass Tuba and Piano

San Antonio, TX: Southern Music Co., 1962.
Movements: I. Allegro con moto
                II. Allegretto con grazioso e espressivo
                III. Allegro con brio
Instrumentation: Tuba and Piano

This sonata was first published by the Interlochen Press and was later transferred to Southern Music Co. It is one of the finest written works in the entire tuba repertoire. It is a work of major proportions that is entirely constructed within the practical tonal range of the large CC or BB♭ tuba. Dr. Beversdorf was not only a composer of national repute but also a trombonist and tubist of professional calibre. It is only natural that a tuba sonata by him should be a guide by which other composers can determine what is and what is not idiomatic for the bass tuba.

The first movement, "Allegro con moto," is very rhythmic and driving. The meter changes involve 4/4, 2/4, 3/4, and 5/4. The introduction and the first theme are very forceful and *marcato*, involving sixteenth-note runs and strong accents. The player will find complete control of double-tonguing technique very helpful in this movement. The interval of a fourth is encountered quite often. The second theme is very lyrical and played legato—the tempo must remain the same as the first theme. This second theme is composed basically of scalewise motion. The development section begins with snatches of the first theme transposed at different levels, and from there to the end, it alternates between the material of the two themes, ending with basically the same figure with which the tuba entered. There are rhythmic, articulative, and flexibility difficulties that require a mature player for an effective performance of this first movement.

The second movement, "Allegretto con grazioso e espressivo," is in 4/4 with one measure of 2/4 and one of 5/4. It begins with the tuba alone and ends with the piano alone. It is basically in ABA form, with the A section very legato and sustained, and the B section more dramatic. The A section returns with its flowing lines of eighth notes and works its way down to F^2. This movement demands a high degree of musical maturity and tonal control that is not fully apprehended by just looking over the part.

The third and last movement, "Allegro con brio," is basically in 6/8, with two sections in 2/4 and a silent measure in 3/8. This staccato, rhythmically driving movement requires a very facile tongue and a quick mind. It should be taken at the fastest tempo that one can comfortably single-tongue. Above all, one should not underrate the dynamic levels in this movement, but always remember that they are relative and that "piano" is not supposed to be the lowest level that one can play. There are no rhythmic problems encountered in this movement other than the tempo at which they are executed and a few cases of duplets.

The first problem to be faced by the tuba player who would like to perform this work is to find a first-rate pianist, because the accompaniment can be performed by no one less.

Program note by R. Winston Morris, Professor of Music at Tennessee Tech University, Cookeville, TN.

John Boda (b. 1922)

John Boda is Professor of Music at Florida State University, Tallahassee, FL.

Sonatina for Tuba and Piano

North Easton, MA: Robert King Music Co., 1968.
Movements: I. Quarter note = 80
                II. Quarter note = 112
Instrumentation: Tuba and Piano

Movement I of *Sonatina for Tuba and Piano* is in three distinct
sections. Section I shows the tuba as a grotesque personality;
angry, with no compromise (jagged short motives, dissonant
harmonies). Section II is calmer and more lyric; it has more
diatonic lines, with rising piano lines. Section III returns to the
first section sounds, ending on a strong dissonance.

Movement II displays the tuba as a clown or comic. Section
I is a playful dance over a piano ostinato. In Section II the right
hand of piano joins the tuba in playful dancelike motives. In
Section III the first movement sounds return to interrupt the
dance, which leads to an unaccompanied tuba cadenza (in contrast to the strict rhythm of the dance). Themes recur in
reverse order after the cadenza (Section II and then Section I).
They are again interrupted by sounds from the first movement.
This time there is a release of tension (major triads in the
piano), and the movement comes to a quiet, peaceful end.

Doug Borwick (b. 1952)

Doug Borwick is Associate Professor of Arts Management at
Salem College, Winston-Salem, NC.

Tuba Sonata

Winston-Salem, NC: Doug Borwick, 1982.
Movements: I. Recitative and Aria
                II. Theme and Variations
                III. Rondo
Instrumentation: Unaccompanied Tuba

Tuba Sonata was written in 1982 as part of a series of works for unaccompanied instruments. Each piece in the series was designed to explore the technical as well as the musical capabilities of the instrument. The series was also part of the process which led me to a full-blown lyric, tonally based style. The choice of tuba for one of the first of these pieces was due to my pleasure at the result of an earlier theatre piece for tuba, *Tuba Mirum*, written in the early '70s.

All three movements are structurally tonal. Movement I, "Recitative and Aria," has a straightforward introduction, recitative, ABA[1] aria, and a codetta. Movement II consists of a theme based on a transposition of the BACH motive, nine progressively more complex variations, and a brief coda. This movement includes some extended techniques—unpitched tongue clicking and hummed accompaniments to the played line. (The humming is designed to be appropriate for male or female performers.) Movement III, "Rondo," incorporates thematic material of the first two movements in an ABACABA form.

Bruce Broughton (b. 1945)

Bruce Broughton is a governor of the Academy of Motion Picture Arts and Sciences. He teaches film composition at the University of Southern California and is a lecturer at the University of California—Los Angeles. His credits include *Honey, I Blew Up the Kid*, *The Rescuers Down Under*, *Silverado* (the soundtrack of which was nominated for a Grammy), and *Young Sherlock Holmes*. He has won six Emmy awards for his work in television, which includes the scores for *Dinosaurs*, *Tiny Toon Adventures*, and *How the West Was Won*.

Concerto for Tuba and Wind Orchestra

New York: Kalmus Music, Inc., 1978.
Movements: I. Allegro moderato
                         II. Andante moderato (Aria)
                         III. Allegro leggero
Instrumentation: Tuba and Wind Orchestra or Tuba and Piano

Concerto for Tuba and Wind Orchestra, conceived originally as
a *Sonata for Tuba and Piano* (in which form it also exists), was
composed in 1978 for Tommy Johnson and myself. At that
time we had been performing a great deal together. One of our
programs was a brass quintet recital in which each of the members also performed a solo work. Most of the music played was
neither deep nor even very good, but it was all a great deal of
fun, due in some part to the informal nature of the evening.
Wishing to have something that was as enjoyable to listen to as
it was to perform, I decided to write a piece for us. The result
was the *Sonata.* The reception to the piece was good from the
start. So in order to expand the opportunities for performance,
I decided to arrange it as a concerto (the soloist's part is the
same) for orchestral winds, percussion, harp, and keyboard. In
this way the piece could be played with either an orchestra or
a symphonic wind ensemble. As it turned out, the *Concerto*
became a band piece. It is possible that at some time in the
future it will appear in a full orchestral version.
      The first movement begins with an insistent motif in the ac-
companiment, which is eventually used as a background to the
soloist's theme. The tuba avoids playing the accompanying
figure—which is used as a unifying device throughout the
movement—until the very end, when it is played almost as an
afterthought. The second movement was inspired by a trombone piece played on the aforementioned quintet recital, in
which the accompaniment was a series of half-step progressions.
The "Aria" title is not entirely serious, but the piece has to be
performed as though it were. The final movement begins with a
flurry of activity in the accompaniment, actually a compressed
version of the bouncy theme which the tuba will soon play, and
the two protagonists drive the piece relentlessly to the end.

Newel Kay Brown (b. 1932)

Newel Kay Brown is Professor of Composition and Theory at the University of North Texas, Denton, TX.

. . . and then there were six

New York: Seesaw Music Publishers, 1978.
Movements: I. Theme and Vision
              II. Contemplation
             III. Joy
              IV. Confrontation
               V. Reconciliation
              VI. Resolution
Instrumentation: Tuba and Piano

This work was written in January 1975 for my friend Gary Bird, who was a student at North Texas State University at the time (the name was recently changed to University of North Texas).

A slow stately theme is announced by the solo tuba, after which the piano introduces the first variation, "Vision," with a series of compound thirds, while the tuba continues to explore and expand perfect fifths from the theme. The second variation ("Contemplation") contrasts long, sustained tuba pitches with close thirds in disjunct patterns of the accompaniment. "Joy," the third variation, is established by a lively 5 + 5 + 4 metrical grouping in which the tuba is given its first lyrical lines.

"Confrontation," the fourth variation, is expressed by repeated accented gestures and faster scale passages by both instruments. Chords in fourths and fifths also add color to the piano part. Blurred, complex harmonies are sustained under a slow, but lyrical line from the tuba in the fifth variation, "Reconciliation." Rapid sixteenth-note passages in the tuba interplay with resolute octaves and open fifths in the accompaniment to bring the sixth variation, "Resolution," to a fitting conclusion.

Robert Chamberlin (b. 1950)

Robert Chamberlin is Associate Professor of Music and Coordinator for Academic Advising at Webster University, St.
Louis, MO.

Daysong

St. Louis, MO: Robert Chamberlin, 1985.
Movements: One Movement
Instrumentation: Tuba, Marimba, Two-channel Tape

Daysong was composed in 1985 for Scott Watson and Mary
Watson on a commission from Scott Watson. They gave the
premiere of the work that year at a new-music festival at the
University of Kansas in Lawrence.

Daysong has no specific program but is intended to be heard
as a daydream, wandering through loose associations from one
thought to another. Some portions of the piece have strictly
measured and timed sequences; at other times, the movement
is much freer and less strictly timed. It is hoped that shifts in
perception of time will enable the listener to make free associations in the manner of a daydream.

Overall, the composition moves from a group of seemingly
disconnected sporadic gestures to a final section based on a pulsating drone (provided by the tape). A variety of coloristic
devices are used with the tuba, in particular, including multiphonics, breathing through the tuba, timbral trills, and
half-valve technique. The sounds on the tape are derived primarily from pipe organ and archifoon (31-tone-per-octave
electric organ).

Elegy for Solo Tuba

St. Louis, MO: MMB Music Inc. (Norruth), 1981.

Movements: One Movement
Instrumentation: Tuba alone. (A grand piano is needed for added resonance.)

Elegy for Solo Tuba was composed in 1981 for Jerry Young. We met as students at the University of Illinois in Urbana-Champaign, and it was there that we developed a strong friendship. Jerry has always been a champion of my efforts as a composer and as a result of this prodding, I composed a trio for tuba, string bass, and harp, called *Avalon*. While at the University of Illinois, Jerry premiered that work and encouraged me to compose for solo tuba.

Elegy was written in 1981 as a response to the assassination of Anwar Sadat. It is an expression of my sadness and anger that people resort to that particular type of violence for political gain. Because it was written as a spontaneous response to the assassination, the actual time spent composing was less than one week. It was an intense effort and a rewarding experience.

I spent three days with Jerry and Dan Perantoni, who was visiting Jerry. I sketched out my ideas, tried out sounds, and received advice from both of them. Composing *Elegy* was one of the best collaborative experiences I have ever had.

In addition to the programmatic content, this composition was an attempt to write a virtuosic piece for tuba, stretching the color potential of the instrument. Probably the most characteristic sound of the piece is the result of playing the tuba into the piano while the pedal is depressed. This creates echo effects that are sometimes very pronounced and at other times quite subtle. A variety of coloristic devices are also employed, including multiphonics, pitch bends, half-valve technique, glissandi, and whispering through the tuba.

Barney Childs (b. 1926)

Barney Childs is Professor of Composition and Music Literature and Director of the New Music Ensemble at the University of Redlands, Redlands, CA.

Mary's Idea for Tuba and Harpsichord

New York: Composers Facsimile Edition, 1967.
Movements: One movement, sectional
Instrumentation: Tuba and Harpsichord

In an early issue of *Brass and Woodwind Quarterly*, editor/reviewer Mary Rasmussen made some comments about the state of tuba and piano literature, wondering why not tuba and harpsichord? I thought this a first-rate suggestion—I have always enjoyed composing for instrumental combinations that some consider bizarre—so I wrote *Mary's Idea*, the title suggested by the jazz piece *John's Idea* rather than anything having to do with lambs. The piece was composed in 1967; the premiere took place at the University of New Hampshire (Ms. Rasmussen's location) on April 1, 1968, with tubist Barton Cummings and harpsichordist Louise Rogers. (I have occasion to remember this concert not only because of the performance; the trip to return the harpsichord in John Rogers's station wagon through foul sleety weather was interrupted by a burnt-out rear wheel bearing.)

The piece runs close to eight minutes. It is a spare and fairly austere work, with complex rhythmic interaction between instruments and occasional separately articulated independent lines. The tuba part combines lyric and declamatory modes, includes large intervals, avoids the extreme register, and requires good control throughout the range. It has no official "form"—I agree with the poet Robert Creeley that "form is what happens"—but a couple of chords reappear from time to time in the harpsichord, like signposts. Both players should know how to handle silences.

The work is inscribed to my friend tubist Lewis Waldeck. Under no circumstances is piano to be substituted for harpsichord!

Seaview for Tuba and Piano

Chicago: M. M. Cole Publishing Co. 1971.
Movements: One movement, sectional
Instrumentation: Tuba and Piano

In 1969 I received a letter from Jan Bach, explaining that a publishing house had asked him to provide new compositions for brass and piano. They were intended for the strong high school or beginning college player and should be properly limited in range and difficulty. Would I do the tuba one? And, if so, would I consider introducing some contemporary approaches in the work? This seemed a first-rate idea, and *Seaview* was the result. It is inscribed to my friend (and one-time composition student) Ray Weisling, in those days himself a tubist. The premiere was at the California College of the Arts on June 18, 1971, by Donald Smith, tuba, and Barry Chamberlain, piano.

The work, about eight minutes long, includes pitch sequences to be articulated into a line, a section in which each performer chooses independently from a group of phrases and determines the order in which they will be played, a short spoken passage, and enough rhythmic variation to test the players' capacity in carrying the rhetoric of the music through shifting stress and gesture. The title's significance can be educed (and has so been occasionally) if one is familiar with a television adventure show of those days which featured a futuristic submarine (the *Seaview*), completely equipped for scientific research. The clue is from the soundtrack: when the ship was cruising about in good order the machinery gave out two constant sounds, each repeating at its own steady rhythm, and this has been evoked on occasion in the piano part. This is simply a musical homage and is in no way programmatic; the fact that the spoken words are from Herman Melville may or may not be coincidental.

A question of summer for Tuba and Harp

New York: Composers Facsimile Edition, 1976.
Movements: One movement, sectional
Instrumentation: Tuba and Harp

A question of summer was commissioned in 1976 by Ivan Hammond, tubist at Bowling Green State University, and his colleague harpist Ruth K. Inglefield. The premiere was at an MTNA conference in Chicago, on May 4, 1978, by tubist Dan Perantoni and harpist Shirley Blankenship.

The work's single movement lasts between nine and ten minutes. The tuba part covers the full range of the instrument (pedal C on the low end; a stepwise altissimo ascent until a note is cracked) and includes special colors and wide intervals. A section in the middle asks each instrument to perform what is written at its own pace—the material evocative of the jazz improvisation of trombonist Roswell Rudd and harpist Alice Coltrane. Returning to the tuba's opening *bel canto* style and the (perhaps ominous) rapping on the harp soundboard, the piece concludes, after what seems to be the final coming to rest, with a single upflung gesture. What may be seen at first as rhythmic problems should provide no obstacle to professionals in projecting the rhetoric of the lines.

The recording of the piece (CRI SD-556) by Mr. Hammond and Ms. Inglefield was made possible by an American Composers Alliance Recording Award.

John Downey (b. 1927)

John Downey is Distinguished Professor of Music, Theory, and Composition at the University of Wisconsin-Milwaukee.

Tabu for Tuba

Brookfield, CT: Mentor Music, 1965.
Movements: One movement, "Lyrical"
Instrumentation: Tuba and Piano

The title turned out to be the most controversial aspect of my composition for tuba and piano! I used the word *Tabu* in the title in a special way, hoping to convey the notion of mystery and the forbidden. I wanted to write a work that was predominantly lyrical in emphasis, with no humorous passages inserted or any kind of the "um-pah-pah" bass notes that one superficially associates with the tuba. In this sense, I felt that what I was trying to do was usually considered taboo for this big, but nonetheless beautiful sounding instrument. The tuba's singing tone is unique!

Another aspect of *Tabu for Tuba* which was particularly challenging was the combination of tuba and piano. The timbral characteristics of these instruments are vastly different so I searched for some kind of approach that could merge their dissimilarities. I hit on the idea of handling them both in a kind of contrapuntal manner, allowing their independent timbral qualities to help differentiate their respective lines.

This four-and-a-half to five-minute composition is in an arch form, tripartite in structure. The return of the first section features an inverted form of the tuba's opening lyrical statement.

This composition was originally written for a tuba-playing theory student of mine at the University of Wisconsin-Milwaukee, Daniel Neesley. He premiered it at our university in the spring of 1967, with Walter Baker at the piano. Through Mr. Neesley's teacher Arnold Jacobs, former principal tuba

player with the Chicago Symphony, the piece was brought to
the attention of tuba virtuoso Harvey Phillips, who quickly
endorsed its publication by Mentor Music, Inc.

Since its premiere, *Tabu for Tuba* has been championed all
over the world by Harvey Phillips. He recorded it for Gasparo
Records in 1986 with the composer at the piano.

Arthur Frackenpohl (b. 1924)

Arthur Frackenpohl is Professor Emeritus of the Crane School
of Music, Potsdam College (SUNY), Potsdam, NY.

Sonata for Tuba and Piano

Delevan, NY: Kendor Publishing Co., 1983.
Movements: I. Fast
                          II. Slowly
                          III. Lively
Instrumentation: Tuba and Piano

My *Sonata for Tuba and Piano* was written for and dedicated
to Harvey Phillips. I had the pleasure of hearing him perform
the *Sonata for Bass Tuba and Klavier* by Hindemith in Bloomington, Indiana, at an international tuba gathering, and Harvey
and I performed my *Concertino for Tuba and Piano* during an
Octubafest in Potsdam, New York. The sonata is a large work
designed to show the lyrical and technical capabilities of the
tuba.

The first movement is in sonata form, the second in song
form, and the last in rondo form. In this composition as well
as in others, I have tried to achieve a proper balance between
the tuba and piano by writing: for the tuba alone (beginning of
second movement), antiphonally (second theme of the third
movement), contrapuntally (development of first movement),

and for the instruments in different registers (second theme of the second movement).

Movement I—Fast (sonata allegro form)
1. First theme (mm. 1–27)—detached, melodic fourths and thirds
2. Transition (mm. 28–32)
3. Second theme (mm. 33–56)—lyrical, melodic sevenths
4. Transition (mm. 57–61)
5. Development (mm. 62–83)—some canonic writing
6. Recapitulation of first theme (m. 84)
7. Recapitulation of second theme (m. 112)
8. Codetta (m. 139)

Movement II—Slowly (song form)
1. First theme—3/4—first statement *poco rubato*
2. Second theme—4/4—a bit faster, uses pentatonic elements and is based on a free melodic inversion of a Southern folk hymn
3. Variation of shortened first theme
4. Variation of shortened second theme
5. Another treatment of the first theme followed by a short coda

Movement III—Lively (rondo form)
1. First theme A (mm. 1–25)—brisk 6/8
2. Second theme B (mm. 26–56)—a more relaxed 6/8
3. First theme A' (mm. 56–84)—in 2/4 this time
4. Third theme C (m. 85–)—legato 9/8, derived from second theme of first movement
5. Extended Coda based on A

Duration: about 13' 20".

Gregory Fritze (b. 1954)

Gregory Fritze is Assistant Chair of Composition and Director of the Wind Ensemble at Berklee College of Music, Boston, MA. He is also principal tubist of the Rhode Island Philharmonic in Providence.

Basso Concertino

Sharon, MA: Gregory Fritze, 1984.
Movements: One movement in sections—slow, fast, slow, fast
Instrumentation: Solo Tuba with Brass Quartet (two trumpets, horn, and trombone)

Basso Concertino was composed in 1984 to provide a brass quintet piece featuring the tuba. The tuba part is very difficult, with a range of four octaves, C^2 to c^1; while the other brass parts are less difficult. I hoped to feature the tuba in a virtuosic manner without causing difficulties for the other brass players. The piece has been performed many times with only one ensemble rehearsal.

The tuba begins alone, playing a long expressive melody, which is the basis of the composition. The melody is developed in counterpoint with the other instruments and culminates with the tuba playing a three-note motif from the melody in the extreme high register.

A faster section begins with a rhythmic and slightly melodic variation of the opening theme. This melody is developed and builds up to a frenzy, after which there is a long tuba cadenza. After the cadenza, the first slower section is brought back before the final buildup of the faster rhythmic theme, rising to the tuba note of c^1. The tuba then ends with a pedal C^2 four octaves below.

The piece was premiered by Gregory Fritze and the Thundermist Brass Quintet and The Berklee Performance Center in March 1985. It was recorded by the Cambridge Symphonic Brass Ensemble on the Crystal Record label. The total duration of the piece is nine minutes.

A version with synthesizer was arranged in 1987. It has several sounds (or patches) that can be used. The sounds Warm Bell, HarpsiWire, Pipe Organ, etc., were produced with a Yamaha DX7 synthesizer. Similar sounds can be attained on any synthesizer. When the piece was orchestrated especially for keyboard, several textures were changed from the brass version. It was premiered by Gregory Fritze, tuba, and Diana Jackson, synthesizer, at the University of Rhode Island on March 25, 1988.

Sonata for Tuba and Piano

Movements: I. Quarter note = 60, 96, meno mosso, 96
II. Cantabile, espressivo
III. Allegro non troppo
Instrumentation: Tuba and Piano

Sonata for Tuba and Piano was written in 1976. It is dedicated to F. Chester Roberts, former principal tubist with the Pittsburgh Symphony and the Cleveland Orchestra. The range is two octaves and a tritone, from E^2 to B♭.

The first movement is based on a twelve-tone row that is presented in the first twelve notes of the tuba, during which the piano presents several motivic ideas that are used in both the piano and the tuba throughout the movement.

The second movement is based on the cantabile style of the *bel canto* set to an atonal framework. Roberts used the *bel canto* as a very important part of his tuba teaching.

The third movement is a bit programmatic, similar to the story of *Tubby the Tuba*. It first depicts the tuba playing an umpah pattern, but it gets tired of that and starts to add more notes. The piano yells at the tuba player, saying that tubas are only supposed to play umpahs. The tuba then starts yelling at the piano, saying that tubas can play all kinds of music, not just umpahs. The piano plays a cadenza, which shows the frustration of having to play with a tuba. The tuba then plays a cadenza. In this soliloquy, the tuba complains of not having the opportunity to be recognized for its own self. The piano then plays the umpah by itself, with the tuba interrupting. The feuding continues. The tuba and piano then try to apologize to each other, but the feud continues to the end with a tuba glissando "rip" over the entire register, E^2 to B♭.

The piece was premiered by John Cole at Indiana University in 1977. The length of the entire piece is twelve minutes.

Yevrah Yad Thrib Bypah

Sharon, MA: Gregory Fritze, 1979.

Movements: I. Slow and Dramatic
                II. Lento, Rubato
                III. Dancelike
                IV. Allegro non troppo
Instrumentation: Tuba alone

Yevrah Yad Thrib Bypah was composed in 1979 for the birthday
of Harvey Phillips. The title spells "Happy Birthday Harvey"
backwards—almost. A twelve-tone row is the basis of all the
movements. It is about 95 percent strict twelve tone—notes
were changed here and there to make it more musical, just as
"Yppah" was changed to "Bypah." The range is three octaves
and a perfect fourth, C^2 to f.

The first movement encompasses dramatic contrasts in
dynamics, rhythm, and register. These include vast *crescendos*
and subito *pianissimos* after *crescendos*, angular melodies
encompassing the entire range of the tuba, and very long sustained notes adjacent to fast rhythmic motives.

The second movement continues many of the dramatic contrasts of the first, but adds the use of a long note trill starting
with a *sforzando piano*, then a *crescendo*, then *diminuendo* to
piano. This movement is more thematic than the motivic first
movement. The movement ends with a very slow melody in
the extreme low register and ends on a pedal C^2.

The third movement is in the character of a scherzo. The
meter is 3/8 with sudden changes to 2/4, which highlight the
tritone notes f to b. Multiphonics are used to give a feeling of
two-voice counterpoint. The movement ends with a three-
octave glissando "rip" from F^2 to f.

The fourth movement is based on a repeating-note (C) pattern outlining the thematic rhythmic pattern of 4/4 plus 3/4.
This rhythmic theme is interspersed with melodic interrup-
tions. Tapping metal on metal (usually one ring on the tuba),
popping the mouthpiece, and multiphonics are used to bring
back the rhythmic theme. The coda contains material from
previous movements; the final ending is a glissando "rip"
down from b to C^1.

The piece was premiered at Berklee College of Music in
February 1981. The length of the entire work is approximately
seven minutes.

Crawford Gates (b. 1921)

Crawford Gates is Professor Emeritus and Artist in Residence at Beloit College, Beloit, WI. He has been music director of the Beloit/Janesville Symphony Orchestra and the Rockford Symphony Orchestra.

Suite for Tuba, Op. 53

Beloit, WI: Pacific Publications, 1978.
Movements: I. Intrada
               II. Allemande
               III. Courante
               IV. Sarabande
               V. Gavotte
               VI. Gigue
Instrumentation: Tuba and Chamber Ensemble (Celesta, Harp, Piano and two Percussionists)

This work was written in 1977 on invitation from Cherry Beauregard, Professor of Tuba at the Eastman School of Music of the University of Rochester, who was preparing a faculty recital to be given in Kilbourn Hall in February 1978. He specifically asked me not to write for tuba and piano, as he felt there were already many works available for that combination, and he wanted this work to have a different texture. I tried to imagine a supporting instrumental texture that would be as different as possible from the tuba timbre, and came up with the celesta, harp, piano (third in importance), and a multitude of percussion. The percussion was originally conceived as being performed by one player, but it took two to do the premiere at Eastman and at least two in all other performances since.

Beauregard not only gave a brilliant premiere of this work, supported by colleagues on the Eastman faculty, but also placed it at the conclusion of his recital, where it served as a climax. Many of his outstanding student tubists have played the piece at their own graduate recitals and beyond.

The work is fifteen minutes long and is in six movements, each titled after a baroque dance. I have borrowed not only the dance titles from that period but also the rhythmic germ of each dance. With that starting point, the work otherwise retains its general twentieth-century flavor. Each movement is couched in some instrumental combinations and colors unique to itself and to no other movement.

The first movement, "Intrada," is a kind of tuba improvisation, exploring both low and high registers in close proximity. The surrounding polytonal colors tend to sound vaguely impressionistic.

In the second movement, "Allemande," the supporting colors are made by combining bell tree and gourd in the percussion pallette, along with harp and piano (no celesta here). The harmonic base is tonal, the spirit buoyant and happy. In the interior there is a bravura sixteenth-note scamper that is a challenge, requiring tongue and lip dexterity more usually heard on a piccolo. But it creates lots of fun!

The third movement, "Courante," is largely a duet between tuba and xylophone, although some punctuation is provided by two sizes of triangles and two sizes of suspended cymbals.

The fourth movement, "Sarabande," is a slow, Romantic kind of melody, smooth and sustained, including some excursions into higher lyric register. This is a contemplation. The accompanying trio consists of harp, celesta, and glockenspiel.

In the fifth movement, "Gavotte," the tuba argument is quite angular and rhythmically athletic. The accompaniment is drums (four timpani, four tom toms, and tambourine) and temple blocks.

For the last movement, "Gigue," the form is song with trio. The song is accompanied by celesta, harp, piano, and glockenspiel—the last chattering away in glittering color. The song is in fast gigue rhythm, unabashedly in G major, bright and open-faced. In the trio the triangle replaces the glockenspiel, and the tempo slows down to invoke a kind of lullaby. The gigue in full sail returns with even more gaiety, and the romp ends with the tuba hitting a four-octave jump from a pedal G^3 (off the piano keyboard) to g above middle c.

Thom Ritter George (b. 1942)

Thom Ritter George is Professor of Music at Idaho State University in Pocatello. He is also music director and conductor of the Idaho State Civic Symphony.

Concertino for Tuba, CN 320

Pocatello, ID: Thom Ritter George, 1984.
Movements: I. Allegro ma non troppo
                II. Cantabile e simplice
                III. Vivace
Instrumentation: Tuba and String Orchestra or Tuba and Wind Ensemble or Tuba and Piano

Thom Ritter George's *Concertino for Tuba* was the result of an unusual conducting experience in the spring of 1984. The composer was the conductor for an orchestral concert featuring a tuba soloist. The young player had chosen a work for tuba and string orchestra. At rehearsal, it became obvious that the tuba part was well written and effective but that the string writing was highly unidiomatic. Despite extensive rehearsal the string orchestra music never sounded convincing.

The event prompted Thom Ritter George to think about an original composition for tuba and string orchestra. Strings can be an excellent accompanying medium for solo tuba. The character of the tuba tone is well delineated from that of the string choir. Since George is both a conductor and a string player, it would certainly be possible to invent idiomatic music for strings.

Thinking back to his *Concerto for Flute* (1966), the composer decided to create the music that could also be accompanied by piano and wind ensemble. Like the earlier *Concerto for Flute*, the music would be "original" in all three versions. The advantage of planning three different accompaniments is that none of them would be a transcription of another. All could be made idiomatic for their respective media. Therefore, the *Concertino for Tuba* was in fact written with three original accompaniments: piano, string orchestra, and wind ensemble.

Concertino form seemed best for the work. A concertino is nothing more than a "little concerto," little in the sense that it is brief in duration. The normal fast—slow—fast movement pattern found in many concertos was followed.

The first movement ("Allegro ma non troppo") is cast in a highly abbreviated sonata allegro form. All the customary sections of sonata allegro form were compressed into its 77 measures: Exposition (Theme I and Theme II), Development, Recapitulation (Theme I and Theme II), and Coda. The tuba shows its lyric nature in the music of Theme II; elsewhere, the tuba writing is more animated, often employing leaps and lip slurs. The movement ends quietly.

The second movement ("Cantabile e simplice") is written in three-part song form. The A sections are lyric, asking the player to display good phrasing and musicality. The B section introduces an ostinato in the accompaniment, which accompanies the solo tuba's descent from the upper to the lower part of the bass staff. The movement ends quietly on low B♭, with sustained chords in the accompaniment.

The final movement ("Vivace") again employs sonata allegro form. Since the development is exclusively concerned with material derived from Theme I, it seemed best to recapitulate the themes in reverse order. This allowed the Theme I to appear near the end and lead smoothly to the Coda. The meter is a spirited 6/8. The notes of the principal theme are the same as those used in the principal theme of the first movement: repeated Fs, E♭, C, F. Also, as in the first movement, there are leaps and lip slurs for the solo tuba. The third movement travels through a wide range of keys, many more than are found in the earlier movements. This creates a harmonic excitement which complements the fast tempo and rhythmic excitement of the finale.

The *Concertino for Tuba* has been widely played, both in the United States and abroad, since its composition.

Sonata for Tuba and Piano, CN 307

Pocatello, ID: Thom Ritter George, 1980.
Movements: I.   Vivace e con brio
                      II. Vivace assai
                      III. Ballad: Mesto
                      IV. Ben ritmato
Instrumentation: Tuba and Piano

Thom Ritter George's *Sonata for Tuba and Piano* was composed from March 19, 1980 to June 26, 1989 in Quincy,
Illinois. The *Sonata* is part of the composer's longtime project
of writing a solo sonata for every orchestral instrument. The
work was written for Daniel Perantoni, an outstanding tuba
artist and the composer's friend since their student days in the
early 1960s at the Eastman School of Music.

The actual precomposition process for this *Sonata* and
others in George's sonata series stressed two important fac-
tors: the formal design was planned first, before looking for
specific musical content; and the musical personality of the
solo instrument was studied very carefully so that its resources could be evaluated for musical potential.

Most skilled musicians realize that the individual movements of a multimovement piece should have common
elements which bind it together. At the same time, these
movements should provide contrast within the composition.
It makes sense to plan the general outlines of the whole
composition before looking for specific notes, themes, harmonies, and rhythms. This assumes that the composer views
composition as a structure, much like building a house. Of
course, other composers search for specific musical materials
first and then see how these ideas are best organized for satisfactory musical results. In both cases, composers are trying to
bring the musical form and music content into the best relationship for the piece at hand.

Thom Ritter George most often uses the first of these methods, outlining a form and choosing the number, tempo, and
mood of individual movements. Important key relationships

are chosen at this point, since they have a powerful effect in the musical outcome. After this groundwork is done, the composer begins the search for musical ideas that will best carry out the plan. George has always found the creation of musical ideas to be the easiest part of the work. Commonly many themes and motives are invented before he settles on the most suitable for a specific section. It is most important to devise ideas which have the capability of development, ideas which can display more than one personality. For example, sketches for the first movement of the *Sonata for Tuba and Piano* show some forty measures of thematic material which was worked out and finally rejected in favor of the music which forms the finished version. None of the music in the initial sketch seemed to have the right development potential, exactly the right focus and forward drive to implement the overall plan which had been devised in the precomposition stage.

Evaluating the particular characteristics of the tuba was the other necessary precomposition task. One feature of the instrument is its historic role, that of a slow-moving, fatherly musical personality in the orchestra and band. It is a personality of considerable authority, and it is probably the predominating personality envisioned by Hindemith in writing his famous *Tuba Sonata*. But given recent improvements in the instrument and especially the dramatic advances in playing the tuba, this role has changed. In the hands of a fine artist, the tuba can have considerable agility, a sense of humor, and a good expressive range. The natural tone production of the instrument is somewhat diffuse in character, and this should be taken into account when writing for the tuba. Also, a composer who wishes to make a real contribution to the repertoire should provide new ways of looking at the instrument through the music composed for it.

The first movement ("Vivace e con brio") employs the more agile aspects of the tuba's musical resources. Here we find extensive use of leaps, with the piano commenting on the boisterous motives of the solo part. The music is cast in sonata allegro form, each theme and section being brief in duration. George chooses to de-emphasize the weight of the first movement in relation to the others. Unlike composers of the

Classical and Romantic schools, he prefers to shift the emotional and musical weight of the music to points later in multimovement works. He feels this gives better balance to the work as a whole. The ending of the first movement suggests that "more is to come," rather than "here we are at a great musical moment in the composition."

The second movement ("Vivace assai") is a quick-moving scherzo, probably a distant descendant of the composer's scherzo in his *Brass Quintet No. 1*, written in 1965. In the *Sonata for Tuba and Piano*, the scherzo is written in ABABA structure, a form beloved by Beethoven and used in many of his important compositions. Here the music is playful. The piano's characteristic motive is a *forte* eighth note followed by two *piano* eighths. The tuba has somewhat different music, again using leaps and playing in longer phrases. The B section trios seem quite sustained by contrast, but the forward motion is always continued. Each return of the A and B sections is written out since each return is shorter than the previous version.

The theme of the third movement ("Ballad: Mesto") is the old American folk song "Brave Wolfe," of which the first stanza reads:

> Bad news has come to town, bad news is carried,
> Some say my love is dead, some say he's married.
> As I was a-pondering on this, I took to weeping,
> They stole my love away while I was sleeping.

The modal, melancholy nature of the theme is attractive in its own right and makes a striking contrast to the animated characters of the other movements. The tuba begins alone and muted. The composer is partial to muting brass instruments in lyric movements to provide a change in tone color. The theme itself provides constant and fluid shifts between 3/4 and 4/4, as each line of the text is sung. This feature is retained in the *Sonata*, and the third movement is the expressive center of the work. The mood is further enhanced by the use of A♭ as the tonal center for the Aeolian mode theme. A♭ stands in a minor subdominant relationship to the outer movements. There is an individual color to this key (seven flats) which is very unlike others using white-key notes. This slow movement is in variation form with all the variations being quiet and lyric.

The *Sonata* ends with a fast dance ("Ben ritmato") similar in character to other finales for brass instruments found in George's works. Since many different meters are used (4/4, 7/8, 6/8, 3 + 3 + 2/8, etc.), the composer has not written a time signature. Instead, the music is organized by measure lines for the convenience of the players, who are asked simply to play the notes and rhythms they find in each measure.

This final movement is organized in sonata allegro form, but the first and second themes appear in reverse order during the recapitulation. Interestingly, both themes are fast and hard-driving. In this movement, the piano asserts itself more strongly than in the other movements and has more direct interplay with the musical ideas presented initially by the tuba.

Particular attention has been given to the Coda. It follows closely on the heels of the recapitulated and shortened first theme, rounding off the finale but also providing a brilliant conclusion for the *Sonata* as a whole.

Daniel Perantoni has recorded Thom Ritter George's *Sonata for Tuba and Piano* for Mark Records.

Jennifer Glass (b. 1944)

Jennifer Glass is Professor of Musicianship and Pianoforte at the Guildhall School of Music and Drama, The Barbican, London.

Sonatina for Tuba and Piano

Ampleforth, Yorkshire: Emerson Edition, 1979.
Movements: I. Allegro non troppo
              II. Lento
              III. Tempo di valse
              IV. Presto
Instrumentation: Tuba and Piano

In 1962, as a fresher at Cambridge University (England), I met fellow student John Fletcher, a third-year Natural Sciences undergraduate, but above all a brilliant tubist. I jumped at the opportunity of writing this *Sonatina* for him. I brought it back to college with me at the end of Easter vacation, 1963. He had given me several very useful pieces of practical advice and seemed happy with the result.

We performed it at the University, and again in the late 1960s, as a part of several programs of the Philip Jones Brass Ensemble, including a BBC broadcast in 1968. John, by that time principal of the London Symphony Orchestra, recorded it with pianist Michael Reeves in Japan while on tour there in 1980 (K28C-65). Alas, he died in 1987. Other tubists had picked it up after its rather late publication, most notably Ron Bishop of the Cleveland Orchestra.

There is little to say of the four movements of my *Sonatina* that would not be obvious to anyone with ears. It develops and repeats material as any organized music will. The tuba and piano parts are of equal importance and were conceived as a unity. The "Lento" bore the description "unashamedly romantic" in the 1963 program note, mainly for the reason that Cambridge in the 1960s was all for Monteverdi and Stockhausen but turned a deaf ear to the rest. The enlightened few sat huddled in corners around Tschaikovsky, Puccini, Mahler—but it was difficult to write a movement like the little "Lento" and have it taken seriously. The "Tempo di valse" quotes Beethoven's Diabelli theme, and the "Presto" was an item for John Fletcher's steam train collection.

Morton Gould (b. 1913)

Morton Gould is a conductor and has served as president of ASCAP. A prolific and versatile composer, he has written in a wide range of genres but is best known for his orchestral works, which include concert pieces as well as scores for radio

(Second American Symphony, 1938), Broadway musicals
(*Billion Dollar Baby*, 1945), ballets (*Fall River Legend*, 1947),
film (*Windjammer*, 1958), and television ("Holocaust," 1978).

Tuba Suite for Solo Tuba and Three Horns

New York: G. Schirmer, Inc., 1971.
Movements: I. Prelude
               II. Chorale
               III. Waltz
               IV. Elegy
Instrumentation: Tuba and three Horns

This composition is dedicated to the memory of William Bell
and was written in August 1971 on the invitation of Harvey
Phillips to honor our mutual friend and much admired colleague. Bell was one of our great artists, and he made many
recordings and performances with me. Subsequently, when
Bill retired, Harvey also played my sessions. Shortly after
William Bell's death, I received a call one late evening at a
time when I was desperately trying to keep up with a commission deadline. It was Harvey calling, urgently requesting me to
do a work for tuba in memory of Bill Bell.

The last thing I wanted to get involved with, because of other
pressures, was a work for tuba. However, Harvey was most per-
suasive, and after some "telephone arm-twisting" I agreed. The
next problem was—what kind of piece? I finally decided on a
texture that would involve the tuba and some relatives,
namely, three French Horns. The work has been recorded by
Harvey Phillips.

The *Suite* is self-evident in its texture and titled movements.
The tuba has a wide range of expression and dynamics far
beyond the restrictive roles usually assigned to it. The movements of the *Suite* use the extensive registers of the instrument
with their respective timbres, breaking out of often low-register
containment. The general character is lyrical and employs the
tuba as a mellifluous singing and "light" moving virtuoso
instrument.

I hope it is a contribution to the literature and gives musical recognition to the tuba's importance in the sound of music.

Edward Gregson (b. 1945)

Edward Gregson is Senior Lecturer in Music at Goldsmiths College, University of London, and Professor of Composition at the Royal Academy of Music, London.

Concerto for Tuba and Brass Band
(Orchestra, Band, Piano)

Sevenoaks, Kent: Novello and Co., Ltd., 1978.
Movements: I. Allegro deciso
               II. Lento e mesto
               III. Allegro giocoso
Instrumentation: Tuba and Brass Band (Orchestra, Concert Band, Piano)

My *Tuba Concerto* was written for my dear friend John Fletcher, now sadly no longer with us. I had promised for some time to write him a major work, and in 1975 the opportunity came when Besses o'th' Barn Band (one of the oldest brass bands in Britain and also one of the most enterprising) had the idea of commissioning a concerto for tuba and brass band. This was a difficult task, mainly because of the problems of balance in such a medium. I wanted to produce a work which was accessible for audiences, although I was distinctly aware that such a combination was difficult enough without making the music highly modernistic. Also I wanted to exploit the lyrical characteristics of the tuba, which I hope I have done. Essentially I wanted to write a piece of music that would stand the test of time.

It was duly performed on April 24, 1976 in Middleton,

Manchester, with John Fletcher, tuba, and the Besses o'th' Barn Band conducted by the composer. André Previn was present at the premiere, as he was making a documentary for BBC Television on his discovery of the British Brass Band.

A couple of years later I set about making a version for orchestra. It was given its premiere by John Fletcher with the Scottish National Orchestra conducted by Sir Alexander Gibson at the 1983 Scottish Proms in Edinburgh. This is my favorite version, as its clarity of texture and lush string sound set off the tuba in a much more effective manner. The slow movement in particular comes off much better.

My publisher then wanted me to do a version for wind band. John Fletcher again gave the first performance of this in Grieg Halle, Bergen, Norway, in June 1984. Thus there are three different performing versions of the concerto (indeed four if you count the version for tuba and piano, which I made at the original time of its composition). I have been particularly pleased that this *Concerto* has received so many performances throughout the world and has been played by so many eminent tuba players.

The *Concerto* is in three movements, following the usual quick—slow—quick pattern: "Allegro deciso," "Lento e mesto," "Allegro giocoso." The first is in a sonata form shell with two contrasting themes, the first rhythmic, the second lyrical. There is a reference made in the development section to the opening theme of Vaughan Williams's *Tuba Concerto*, but only in passing. The second movement unfolds a long cantabile melody for the soloist, which contrasts with a ritornello idea which is announced three times by the band/ orchestra. The last movement is in rondo form, alternating the main theme with two episodes. The first of these is a broad sweeping tune, the second is jazzlike. After a short cadenza, reference is made to the opening of the *Concerto*, and the work ends with a triumphal flourish.

Walter S. Hartley (b. 1927)

Walter S. Hartley is Professor of Music at the State University of New York at Fredonia.

Sonata for Tuba and Piano

Bryn Mawr, PA: Theodore Presser Co., 1967.
Movements: I. Andante—Allegro agitato
                II. Allegretto grazioso
                III. Adagio sostenuto
                IV. Allegro moderato, con anima
Instrumentation: Tuba and Piano

This work is based on a twelve-tone row which is treated thematically rather than serially, with much imitative counterpoint. It has been played by many tubists, including Harvey Phillips, Rex Conner, Rudolph Emilson, Robert LeBlanc (who recorded it for Coronet), and Peter Popiel.

[The following material is extracted from an article by Peter Popiel in the April 1970 issue of *Instrumentalist*.] Peter Popiel is Professor of Music, teaching Tuba, Euphonium, Music History, and Literature at the Crane School of Music, State University of New York at Potsdam.

Hartley's ideas relating to composition for the tuba are valuable and intriguing, offering a much-needed perspective both to the player and to the potential composer.

The Tuba as solo instrument, or as soloist in an ensemble, should essentially and ideally be a melodic bass. It is particularly suited to obbligato (melodic accompaniment of another melody) or other contrapuntal treatment. A good source of inspiration for tuba-writing should be the pedal parts in J. S. Bach's organ works, particularly the Trio Sonatas. The most generally useful melodic range in tubas (contrabass tubas in CC or in BB♭) is A^2 to

A; the high baritone and contrabass register should be used sparingly, especially for younger players, although for the sake of variety they should not be avoided in serious work. Melodies conceived for higher register instruments or voices, particularly in the soprano range, tend to be unsatisfactory, for reasons of harmonic balance, when transcribed for the tuba. Spacing should always be carefully handled, especially between the tuba and other low winds, to achieve good coloristic balance. The tuba tone has fewer strong high partials than other brass instruments, particularly horn and trumpet. This must be borne in mind when associating these colors.[1]

The *Sonata for Tuba and Piano* is one of the composer's most extensive works; it is written in four movements, the last two of which are played without pause. Hartley defines his style as "freely tonal and broadly based on Classical forms." The work opens with a statement of a twelve-tone theme by the solo tuba, a theme which is to appear in conjunction with other themes throughout the entire sonata as a cyclical force. As this theme makes its appearances, it does so in several forms: in its entirety, in truncated form, inverted, in retrograde, transposed, rhythmically transformed, and in various contrapuntal combinations.

This twelve-tone theme is a combination of recitative and cadenza styles, and is typically chromatic; the movement unfolds with another feature of Hartley's style: the disjunct, craggy melodic contour characterized by wide leaps. This same contour occurs soon afterward; this time in *allegro agitato* tempo when the cyclic theme—actually, the first nine notes of it—returns transposed up a major sixth. The final two measures of the movement project notes one to four of the cyclic theme in retrograde, and these four notes foreshadow many interesting events of the next movement.

The last four notes of the first movement form the "head" of a new theme, which makes its appearance in the piano at the opening of the second movement. This theme is a rather extended one, with fifteen measures elapsing before the entrance of the tuba with the same material. This theme, and motives taken from it, pervade the entire movement, which is an *Allegretto grazioso* of scherzolike character. The opening of this movement also demonstrates the expert scoring of tuba with accompaniment; it is evident from the beginning that Hartley has kept the piano left hand out of the register in which the tuba is playing and, in so doing, has avoided the trap into which many composers have fallen—a blurred, murky texture which results when tuba and piano articulate rapid passages in the same register.

The dirgelike third movement again presents the twelve-tone row in its entirety. The movement is built around a gradual and continuous buildup of tension through the use of increased rhythmic activity, rising tessitura, and intensified dynamic levels, reaching a strong and deliberate climax. The climax quickly dissipates into a meditative transition, which leads into the finale.

Articulation becomes a real issue as the final movement opens, and the composer's comments on it are relevant:

> A solo tuba must be extremely well played to avoid untoward associations in the listener (foghorns, large ruminant animals, etc.). Perhaps the most dangerous passage I have written in this respect is the beginning of the Finale of my *Sonata* (1967) which could easily become ridiculous unless lightly and cleanly articulated.[2]

This passage can indeed justify Hartley's fears if the eighth notes in measures 2 and 4 are articulated so fast that they run together, thereby blurring the pitches. At the eleventh measure the piano imitates the opening theme at a twelfth above. The cyclic twelve-tone theme returns in augmentation at measure 54, but utilizes only one through ten of the series, with the eleventh note, G♯, appearing in the piano accompaniment, and the twelfth note, C, in the tuba at measure 60. The movement builds to an exciting *fortissimo* finish, concluding a work which makes considerable demands upon the performer, but which pays generous musical dividends to the player who masters its difficulties and understands its intricacies.

NOTES

1. Walter S. Hartley, in a letter of January 12, 1969 to Peter Popiel.
2. Ibid.

Sonatina for Tuba and Piano

Naperville, IL: Interlochen Press, 1961.
Movements: I. Allegretto
                          II. Largo maestoso
                          III. Allegro moderato
Instrumentation: Tuba and Piano

The *Sonatina* was composed at the suggestion of Rex Conner. When Hartley writes for tuba with accompaniment, his preference is for the piano because he feels that the percussive aspects of that instrument help the tonal distinction. This percussive factor can be seen very clearly in the first movement and would be most difficult to achieve with another accompanying medium.

The second movement is a further illustration of this percussive treatment of the piano, which Hartley emphasizes; it is also a typical texture of which he is fond, particularly in the slow movements: the sustained melodic line supported by thick chordal structures.

Another texture which contrasts with the one above is that involving contrapuntal writing for tuba with piano. Hartley conceives the tuba's accompaniment essentially as a partnership which should contribute musical interest of its own and not merely serve as a backdrop to the solo line. This philosophy pervades many of his works, and a clear example of this contrapuntal partnership occurs in the final movement of the *Sonatina*. The tuba opens the movement with a theme or subject which pivots between C major and the Lydian mode on C via the alternation of the notes F and F♯. This relationship, with its prominent tritone, continues as the piano enters in imitation at the twelfth above four measures later. The imitation is strict, however, only to measure 8, where the third voice enters, and where F and F♯ sound simultaneously after having alternated with each other in close cross-relation for two measures.

Program note by Peter Popiel.

Suite for Unaccompanied Tuba

Bryn Mawr, PA: Elkan-Vogel Co., 1964.
Movements: I. Intrada
            II. Valse
            III. Air
            IV. Galop
Instrumentation: Tuba alone

Hartley defines his style as "freely tonal and broadly based on classical forms." This definition can be applied to the *Suite for Unaccompanied Tuba*. Written in 1962 at the suggestion of Rex Conner, tuba instructor at the National Music Camp, the work is in four movements, each of which is cast in a traditional form.

The "Intrada" (alla marcia) demonstrates Hartley's free application of tonality; the first four measures pass through the keys of G and E♭ and cadence on E. In addition to the freedom of tonality, this typifies the somewhat angular melodic contour of Hartley's tuba writing. Many octaves, fifths, and sevenths are freely used, and even the descending leap of a fourteenth in measure 4 works well on the instrument. The strong accents, sudden dynamic contrasts, and tongue-in-cheek quotations from the typical band "oom-pah" tuba parts combine to make this a most effective movement.

The angular "Valse" opens in B♭, but restlessly moves to D♭ by the fourth measure. The tonal freedom of the first movment is prominent here, particularly in the final twelve measures. Hartley modulates rapidly through the implied keys of A♭, D and A♭, then very suddenly shifts into B♭ for the final cadence.

Program note by Peter Popiel.

Bernard Heiden (b. 1910)

Bernhard Heiden is Professor of Music Emeritus and former Chairman of the Composition Department at Indiana University, Bloomington.

Concerto for Tuba and Orchestra

New York: Peer/Southern, 1979.
Movements: I. Allegro risoluto
              II. Andante
              III. Vivace
Instrumentation: Tuba and Orchestra or Wind Ensemble

There is nothing as inspiring to a composer as a great performer; *Concerto for Tuba and Orchestra* is the second work I have written for Harvey Phillips, my friend and colleague at Indiana University. Under a grant from the National Endowment for the Arts, it was begun in 1975 and finished in 1976, while I was on sabbatical leave in Greece. The first performance took place on November 4, 1977 in Boulder, Colorado by the Boulder Philharmonic Orchestra, Oswald Lehnert conducting, with Mr. Phillips as soloist.

The work follows the traditional concerto form. Soloist and orchestra are treated more or less as equal partners, although most musical ideas are first presented by the tuba. I have tried to show the great range of the instrument, beginning with the opening statement; its flexibility, demonstrated especially in the last movement; but above all, the expressive and lyrical qualities of the tuba, so often forgotten and overlooked by performers and composers. They are most apparent and essential in the slow movement, with its accompanying ostinato figure over which the solo part develops a long melodic line.

In 1980, at the request of Mr. Phillips, I made an arrangement of the work for tuba and wind ensemble which follows the orchestral version exactly. A piano reduction I made is published by Peer International Corp., while score and parts are on rental from the same source.

Variations for Solo Tuba and Nine Horns

New York: Associated Music Publishers, Inc., 1977.
Movements: Theme and Variation Form
Instrumentation: Tuba and nine Horns

John Barrows, eminent hornist, was one of the greatest musicians of our time and a friend and colleague of Harvey Phillips and myself, so when Harvey asked me to compose a piece for a concert dedicated to the memory of John Barrows after his untimely death in 1974, I gladly agreed. There was no condition other than that the work should be for tuba and horns. I chose an ensemble of solo tuba and nine horns, not knowing that this same combination constituted the Valhalla Horn Club, which Barrows had founded in New York City in the 1950s and of which Harvey Phillips was an honorary member (bass horn). The concert took place in Carnegie Recital Hall on January 5, 1975.

The horns are divided into three groups of three players each: numbers one, four, and seven high; two, five, and eight medium; and three, six, and nine low. The work opens with the tuba presenting the first part of the theme against a background of horn sound; the second part of the thematic material consists of echoing horn calls and a short conclusion. Variation I ("Allegro") varies the melodic material of the theme and presents the harmonic content in energetic rhythmic form. Variation II ("Più mosso") exploits the virtuosic quality of the solo instrument. Variation III ("Lento") presents the soloist in a recitative with horns as accompaniment only. Variation IV begins with a canon between a quartet of open horns and quartet of muted horns; it is followed by a dialogue between the solo tuba and the first horn and leads into an extended cadenza for the soloist. The brilliant last variation ("Allegro vivace") contains clusters and cascades of horn sounds and is followed immediately by a Coda in chorale style concluding with a recapitulation of the theme. The work ends quietly, emphasizing the lyrical and intimate character of the music.

The piece is published by Associated Music Publishers and is available on record by Harvey Phillips and the Valhalla Horn Choir, conducted by the composer, on Golden Crest CRSQ 4147.

Paul Hindemith (1895–1963)

Sonate für Bass Tuba und Klavier

Mainz: Schott's Söhne, 1955.
Movements: I. Allegro pesante
                II. Allegro assai
                III. Variationen: moderato commodo
Instrumentation: Tuba and Piano

Between 1936 and 1955, Paul Hindemith composed a series of ten sonatas for various wind instruments and piano: flute (1936), bassoon (1938), oboe (1938), clarinet (1939), horn (1939), trumpet (1939), trombone (1941), English horn (1941), alto horn or saxophone (1943), and tuba (1955).

The *Sonata for Bass Tuba and Piano*, the last work in the series, was completed fully twelve years after the *Sonata for Alto Horn and Piano*. One would correctly assume that a significant stylistic evolution had taken place, setting it apart from its predecessors—and, indeed, from the type of compositional practice generally associated with Paul Hindemith. Throughout these sonatas, and indeed in most of the composer's mature output, one is constantly aware of tonal forces in operation. (It should be mentioned here that the terms "tonal" and "tonality" refer in a largely subjective sense to the presence of a pitch or group of pitches which exert some sort of gravitational pull on the surrounding material.) Despite the fact that one may identify various types of tonal control being employed, the degree to which a perceptible sense of tonality is maintained fluctuates greatly among the sonatas. The *Flute Sonata*, for example, is characterized by clear or fairly clear tonality throughout, whereas the *Sonata for Bass Tuba and Piano* might almost be viewed as a study in extreme and constant chromaticism.

The work requires eleven minutes for performance. The opening movement conforms loosely to sonata form. A two-measure principal theme given exclusively to the tuba is heard in conjunction with a secondary motive found in the piano part. In some ways, the opening passage represents a culmination of experimental tendencies first expressed in earlier works in the series. Most startling is the chromatically saturated melody composed of an eleven-note tone row. Its classic design is broken only by the premature appearance of a second Bb, which serves as a kind of tonal center, insofar as one may be perceived. Some distance above this disjointed melody are streams of broken quartal triads, moving with supreme disregard for even the fleeting tonal implications in the melody. With the extreme contrast in range between piano and tuba and the recurring strong-beat rests punctuating the accompaniment, this passage exhibits a character totally unlike anything in the earlier sonatas in the series. The texture of the accompaniment is percussive, almost glittering, against which the solo tuba may operate without fear of interference.

The second theme consists of two brief motivic ideas, each two measures in length. The second of these is ultimately reshaped into the four-bar subject of the fugato, which constitutes the entire development section. Typically, the imitation used throughout the fugato is of the non-overlapping variety. The Coda, which is also imitative, is likewise based on the second half of the second, or B theme.

The second movement is in an unusual three-part form. The A section consists of two presentations of a nineteen-bar theme, while B is composed solely of continuous repetition by the tuba of a five-bar phrase against varying accompanimental background. Particularly noteworthy is the extraordinary tonal ambiguity created by juxtaposing the ostinato-like tuba part (which consists of nine different pitches) against the inde-

pendent and brilliant, chromatically saturated piano passage
work. The framing tonal center appears to be D♭ (although this
pitch center is militantly disputed by its tritone-related neigh-
bor, A, when the opening theme returns), while the central
section is loosely organized around the pitch of C.

The third movement, entitled "Variationen," corresponds in
many particulars to sonata form, containing recognizable first,
second, and closing themes. The movement opens with a
sparse, two-voiced texture, typical of these sonatas, but developed in this instance to a highly sophisticated degree. While
the tuba presents the principal theme, a two-note accompanying motive evolves, after six statements, into a six-note motive
presented twice, and finally, into a disjunct melody composed
of one-, two-, three-, and four-note fragments. Despite its position as the first statement of a principal theme, the passage is
extremely ambiguous with regard to tonality.

The development section may be divided into five parts,
each approximately as long as the nine-bar principal theme.
Within this section we find free, scherzo-like treatment of
fragments from the first and the second themes, followed by a
contrasting *lento recitativo* suggestive of a lyric cadenza.
Except for a five-bar extension following a brief Coda, the thematic design of the recapitulation is structurally identical to
that of the exposition.

The solo part lies within the capabilities of the "gifted amateur," to which Hindemith frequently makes reference,
although the piano part clearly requires a virtuoso technique.
Of the sonatas in this series, those for brass instruments make
the greatest demands on the keyboard collaborator because of
the extended use of octave and other melodic doublings for purposes of balance.

In that the series of ten sonatas for wind instruments and
piano constitutes an important addition to the literature for
each of the instruments represented, these pieces correspond to
the definition by Hindemith of *Gebrauchsmusik*. He himself
took rather violent issue with those who would apply the term
only to lesser works, easily within the emotional and technical
grasp of the musically uneducated. His attitude is reflected in
a statement made during a lecture entitled "Observations on

Contemporary Music," given at Yale University during the 1939–40 academic year:

> How can we say that just one specific musical style is usable (*brauchbar*)? Shall not every music be usable—a symphony as well as a simple little song? Do not force us into a false standard of musical thought by determining in advance what, under specific circumstances, shall be considered usable regardless of artistic value. Let us rather strive to write a music so good that, with representation suitable to its style, purpose, and instrumentation it must appear completely satisfying and hence, usable.

While Hindemith's approach to composition in general and tonality in particular belongs clearly to the twentieth century, it is nonetheless apparent, particularly in the work under discussion, that his technique springs from a long line of German tradition. His treatment of chromaticism cannot help but bring to mind his immediate predecessors, particularly Max Reger. At the same time, his interest in Classical forms and techniques, also in evidence here, recall a much earlier period. In this respect, Hindemith has successfully reconciled seemingly antithetical attitudes and traditions into a highly personal style, which has frequently been referred to as neo-Classic or, more appropriately, neo-Baroque. Finally, one notes a certain objective quality, even in the tenderest moments in these works. Although highly expressive, they manage to avoid any hint of maudlin sentimentality or self-indulgent expression. In this respect they may be considered as a strong reaction to the excesses of late Romanticism.

The *Sonata for Bass Tuba and Piano* is one of the boldest strokes occurring anywhere in the output of this prodigious composer. It has justly earned a lasting place in the solo repertoire for this noble instrument.

Program note by Dorothy Payne, Head of the Department of Music and Professor of Music Theory at the University of Connecticut at Storrs.

Merle E. Hogg (b. 1922)

Merle E. Hogg is Professor of Music at San Diego State University, San Diego, CA.

Sonatina for Tuba and Piano

Buffalo, NY: Ensemble Publications, 1967.
Movements: I. Allegro
              II. Larghetto
              III. Allegro marcato
Instrumentation: Tuba and Piano

Sonatina for Tuba and Piano was composed in 1963 as a recital piece for the tuba. Ron Bishop, then with the San Francisco Symphony/Opera Orchestra, gave the first performance at San Diego State University in April of that year. He performed it there again, twenty-five years later (when he was a member of the Cleveland Orchestra).

The first movement is cast in the sonata allegro mold. The second movement has a contrasting slower tempo, and it gives the tuba a chance to play with melodic expressiveness.

The last movement used the older rondo form of two contrasting melodic sections between each appearance of the main melodic idea.

Robert Jager (b. 1939)

Robert Jager is Professor of Music and Director of Composition and Theory in the Department of Music and Art at Tennessee Tech University, Cookeville, TN.

Concerto for Bass Tuba and Band

New York: Piedmont Music Co., Inc., 1981.
Movements: One Movement in five distinct sections: Intro-
duction—Dramatic—Reflective—Cadenza-like—Rondino
Instrumentation: Tuba and Band or Tuba and Orchestra or
Tuba and Piano

The *Concerto for Bass Tuba and Band* was composed in 1980
on a commission from Daniel Perantoni and the University of
Illinois. His only request was that the work "not be spacey"
and that it be the kind of piece "that when I stop playing I
want the audience on their feet applauding, and not trying to
leave the hall." To that end, the concerto is written in a neo-
Romantic style.

The original version, accompanied by symphonic band, was
premiered by Mr. Perantoni and the University of Illinois Band
in 1981, with Harry Begian conducting. Subsequently, I made
versions with orchestral accompaniment and piano accompaniment. The latter is published by Edward B. Marks, and the
band and orchestral versions are available on rental from
Theodore Presser.

The work has been recorded by Daniel Perantoni and the
University of Illinois Band. It was also recorded in 1983 by
R. Winston Morris and the Tokyo Kosei Wind Orchestra,
under the direction of the composer. This recording is available through Ludwig Music Company of Cleveland, Ohio.

Roger Kellaway (b. 1939)

Roger Kellaway is a jazz artist, arranger, and composer. He
studied piano, double bass, and composition at the New England Conservatory and has performed with George Shearing,

Jimmy McPartland, Al Cohn, Zoot Sims, Clark Terry, and Bob Brookmeyer. His compositions include film scores (*The Paper Lion*, 1968; *A Star Is Born*, 1976; and *Breathless*, 1983), a ballet (*PAMTGG*, 1971), and the theme music for the TV program "All in the Family."

Songs of Ascent for Solo Tuba and Orchestra

New York: Roger Kellaway, 1989.
Movements: I. Gateway (Introduction; Improvisations 1, 2)
               II. Spirit of the Kingdom (Introduction; Improvisations 3–6)
               III. Desires of the Heart (Improvisations 7–9)
Instrumentation: Solo Tuba and Orchestra

Commissioned by the New York Philharmonic with a grant from Francis Goelet, *Songs of Ascent for Tuba and Orchestra* was written during 1988–89 for Warren Deck, the Philharmonic's principal tubist. It received its premiere on November 24, 1989 in Avery Fisher Hall, in New York, with Warren Deck as soloist and Zubin Mehta conducting. The work, which has a duration of approximately 26 minutes, is scored for an orchestra consisting of three flutes (third = piccolo), two oboes, English horn, two clarinets, bass clarinet, three bassoons, contrabassoon, five horns, two trumpets, three trombones, a large percussion battery, piano, and strings.

From a smile to hysterical laughter is the consistent reaction whenever I mention the tuba. There is no other instrument of the modern orchestra that produces so much instant joy at the sound of its name.

Songs of Ascent is a musical journey, demonstrating the tuba's wide range of melodic and technical skills; at the same time, it is a statement of the tuba's desire to be perceived from a broader perspective. Since childhood, the sound-world of Classical and jazz composition has had a constant fascination for me. *Songs of Ascent*, combining Classical and jazz techniques, was written for Warren Deck and inspired by the encouragement of three other masters of the tuba: Harvey

Phillips, Roger Bobo (of the Los Angeles Philharmonic), and Shemuel Hershko (of the Israel Philharmonic).

Conceptually, *Songs of Ascent* comes closest to the Classical theme-and-variations form. However, in this case the "theme" is represented by an Introduction presenting specific elements of melody, harmony, rhythm, and color—a "song-to-be." The "variations," then, become developments of this material. Moreover, each variation is first designed by harmonic progression (similar to the Baroque figured bass), tempo, and rhythmic cycle. The music above is composed like an improvisation, drawing on material from the Introduction and on the "mood" generated by each tempo, harmonic progression, and rhythmic cycle. Thus, *Songs of Ascent* is revealed as an Introduction with nine Improvisations.

Melody is drawn from four principal motifs, using the following notes: (1) D, G, A; (2) G, A; (3) D, E, F; (4) a tritone in chromatics (seven tones). Harmony is generated from one main "jazz" chord: the minor-thirteenth chord, construction beginning on the note D (Dorian mode) and ascending in alternating minor and major thirds until all seven diatonic tones emerge: D, F, A, C, E, G, B.

The overall structure of *Songs of Ascent* is framed in three harmonic cadences: G major (end of Part I); C major (end of Part II); D major (end of Part III). These cadences—G down to C, up to D—represent the inversion of the first principal melodic motif: D, G, A.

Rhythm is drawn from the numbers 10 plus 11, 15, and 36. (Melodic motif 1 equals 3 and harmonic chord 7 equals 10. Melody 3 plus the inversion within itself—which provides one more new tone—equals 4, adding harmonic chord 7 equals 11. Melody 4 plus its inversion at the octave equals 8, adding harmonic chord 7 equals 15. Thus: $10 + 11 + 15 = 36$.) These four numbers are used to create rhythmic cycles, which, along with their corresponding "harmonic" bass lines and the use of various repeat forms, constitute the architectural basis of *Songs of Ascent*. Within this concept, the numbers 10, 11, and 15 are also used as "time-signatures"—this is related to my work in the middle 1960s with the late Don Ellis, and subsequent studies with Hari Harao, a disciple of Ravi Shankar.

Rhythmic momentum, a necessary element found in any composition integrating jazz techniques, is here generally the responsibility of the "rhythm section"—a quartet of energies comprising piano and/or guitar, double bass, and percussion. Their function is to unite, as one energy, and to assist all other musical elements in achieving total "oneness" (i.e., the entire ensemble performing as one rhythmic energy). To this end, *Songs of Ascent* designates the responsibility of "rhythmic momentum" three different ways: rhythm section—conductor, piano, double bass(es), percussion (Improvisations 2 and 4); tuba soloist (Improvisations 1, 6, and 7); and tuba and rhythm section (Improvisations 3, 5, and 9).

Throughout its journey, the tuba encounters and interacts with many elements from the sound-world of jazz color, such as conga drums; plunger mutes for the bass (inspired by the music of Duke Ellington and notated from a system invented by veteran jazz trombonist Al Grey); various glissandi; a "Jazz-Color Ensemble" (English horn, bass clarinet, bassoon, French horn, two flugelhorns—inspired by the music of Gil Evans). Moreover, the range of color variables in this "sound-palette" is used to place the tuba in many intimate settings (i.e., with string quartet), as well as in the expected full orchestral tutti.

Erland von Koch (b. 1910)

Erland von Koch is Professor of Music at the Royal Swedish Academy of Music. Among his works are five symphonies, twelve concertos, six string quartets, the trilogy *Impulsi-Echi-Ritmi* for orchestra, a chamber opera, an opera for children, five ballets, incidental music for film and television, and eighteen monologues for various solo instruments.

Monologue No. 9

Stockholm: Carl Gehrmans Musikforlag, 1977.
Movements: I. Andante
                II. Allegro vivace
Instrumentation: Tuba alone

My series of eighteen Monologues, from flute to double bass,
began in 1973 with No. 1, for flute, dedicated to Gunilla von
Bahr. They were commissioned by various musicians and published by Gehrmans Musikforlag in Stockholm.

Monologue No. 9 was written in 1975 for the excellent and
admired tuba player Michael Lind, who has recorded it on
GRF Four Leaf Rec. FLC 5045. For Michael Lind I have also
composed *Concerto for Tuba and Strings* in three movements,
1978 (Gehrmans), and *Tubania for Tuba and Piano*, 1983 (MS,
Stockholm: STIM).

A great deal of my music is strongly influenced by Swedish
folk music. The melodic element is most important for me,
and I have learned that the tuba is a wonderful instrument for
melodic and rhythmic compositions, often of virtuosic character. *Monologue No. 9* has two parts: a cantabile and a virtuosic
part ("Allegro vivace").

William Kraft (b. 1923)

William Kraft has had a long association with the Los Angeles
Philharmonic. He was a member of the percussion section for
26 years, eighteen of them as Principal Timpanist; Assistant
Conductor for three years; Composer in Residence; and, since
1981, Director of the orchestra's New Music Group.

Tuba Concerto (Andirivieni)

Van Nuys, CA: New Music West, 1979.
Movements: Sectional
Instrumentation: Tuba with three Chamber Groups and Orchestra

The *Tuba Concerto (Andirivieni)* was first conceived in 1974 in a conversation between Ernest Fleischmann, Roger Bobo, and myself on a bus in Vienna. Mr. Fleischmann suggested that I make a concerto from *Encounters II*, a solo work I had written earlier for Mr. Bobo. The conversation was renewed from time to time and came to fruition when Zubin Mehta asked for a work to mark his final season with the Los Angeles Philharmonic.

The use of *Encounters II* dissolved into a larger conception. I had become very interested in human relationships, specifically with the effect made by those who pass through one's life—friends, colleagues, lovers, mentors, idols, antagonists, and so on. Consequently I became fascinated by the possibility of creating a musical structure in which the character of the tuba would constantly change through interactions with other instruments, which would come and go. Thus the structure of the *Tuba Concerto (Andirivieni)* is one of constantly evolving and changing relationships separated by connective interludes. All this, coupled with Mr. Mehta's leaving the Philharmonic, led to the title *Andirivieni*, which means "coming and going."

After a fairly large orchestral introduction, the tuba is presented in chamber situations with three contrasting quartets, separated by interludes. The first quartet is low-pitched: alto flute, bass clarinet, bassoon, and cello; the second is mid-range: clarinet, English horn, French horn, and viola; the third is high-pitched: piccolo, trumpet, light percussion, and violin. Except for the first, these quartets "come and go"; i.e., they join the tuba in a concertino-like situation. Thus each quartet effects a change in the tuba's character. Each comes and goes. Then the tuba goes (comes) to the brass section and then to the percussion, finally returning to its solo position to function with the entire orchestra.

The pitch formulation of the piece is derived from the inversion of the descending major second marking the entrance of the violins in Mahler's *Ninth Symphony*; and throughout the work, references are made to pieces that exhibit the tuba's potential for beauty, poignancy, and virtuosity, or to pieces of my own, written either for Roger Bobo or with him in mind as a participant. Thus there are quotes from Mahler's *Sixth* and *Ninth Symphonies*, Stravinsky's *Petrouchka* and *Le Sacre du Printemps*, and from my *Encounters II*, *Concerto for Piano and Orchestra*, *Contextures: Riots—Decade '60*, and *Double Trio*, plus a very large reference (in the coda) to my *Concerto for Four Percussion Soloists and Orchestra*. The last reference is large because the performance and recording of that work by the Los Angeles Philharmonic engendered personal as well as professional relationships with Mr. Bobo, Mr. Mehta, and the orchestra that I have deeply cherished these many years.

The *Tuba Concerto (Andirivieni)* was commissioned by Zubin Mehta for Roger Bobo and the Los Angeles Philharmonic and was premiered on January 26, 1978.

Encounters II

New York: MCA Music, 1970.
Movements: Sectional: Slow and dramatic—Presto marcato—Andante—Furioso—Lento e rubato
Instrumentation: Tuba alone

Encounters II was written for Roger Bobo in December 1966 and was premiered at the "Encounters" concert series in Pasadena in 1967.

The first thing Roger and I did was spend a day together, during which we engaged in a creative interplay of ideas and exploration of the instrument's possibilities. The resultant work was, as Roger described it in the liner notes of his second recording of the piece, "higher, lower, faster (probably louder or softer) than any previous work" for tuba.

From the multitude of techniques that evolved, I chose those which I felt were best suited for a piece that was basically expressive along relatively traditional lines. Certain exploratory techniques were eliminated to suit the aesthetics of the piece—an aesthetic in which I wanted to show the truly musical possibilities of the instrument without delving into effects for their own sake.

I wanted the challenge of writing a set of variations for a solo instrument which would create the illusion of accompanying itself, by using various dynamic levels, varying pitch registrations, and especially by utilizing the voice while playing. Much of what resulted was due to Roger Bobo's remarkable virtuosity as well as his creative intelligence.

Frank Lynn Payne (b. 1936)

Frank Lynn Payne is Associate Professor of Theory and Composition at Oklahoma City University.

Canzona de Sonare

Oklahoma City, OK: Frank Lynn Payne, 1982.
Movements: One movement with five continuous sections
Instrumentation: Solo Tuba and Woodwind Quintet

Almost without exception a new composition poses a problem for the composer. If the composition has been commissioned the problem is compounded because the composer's product is tempered by external influences real or perceived. In terms of contemporary ensembles, the string quartet holds the record for longevity. The woodwind quintet and brass quintet are relatively recent additions to instrumental performing groups. These "new" ensembles pose their own particular problems for the composer. But when faced with a deliberate alteration of a semi-established ensemble, such as adding a tuba to the woodwind quintet, the compositional problems and considerations escalate. Before the first note is written the composer must consider whether the added instrument is to be treated as a solo instrument, with the ensemble in an accompaniment position, whether it should be added to the ensemble, or whether one should try to strike some kind of balance between these options. In *Canzona de Sonare* I have opted for the last.

The stereotype of the Classical concerto or similar hybrid of a formalistic approach has, we hope, disappeared from the world of new music. In effectively assimilating a new instrument into an established environment, the composer must create a situation in which the added instrument becomes an integral part of the music. I have tried to apply this principle in the *Canzona de Sonare*. As in any chamber ensemble, each instrument gets its chance, and here the tuba has its moments as a soloist and as a member of the ensemble. Perhaps the tuba should be given more than I have outlined, but that would be introducing a nonmusical essence into a work to the detriment of musical integrity. In composing this work I tried to establish a balance in the ensemble as a whole with the ultimate goal to "make it feel right," i.e., the tuba should feel natural in its surroundings.

The work is in one continuous movement divided into five sections denoted by meter changes (simple to compound) or tempo changes. Ostinato and line constitute the basic building blocks of this work.

Sonata for Tuba and Piano

Delaware Water Gap, PA: Shawnee Press, Inc., 1979.
Movements: I. Fast with energy
            II. Slow and deliberate
            III. Very quick and light
            IV. Fast
Instrumentation: Tuba and Piano

The *Sonata for Tuba and Piano* was written in 1977 for Mark Mordue, tubist with the Oklahoma Symphony Orchestra. The motivation for this work was and continues to be my hope that the lasting music of our time consists of works written for specific individuals or situations and is devoid of the ethnic and political pressures too often found in the major "art centers" of the U.S. The technical accomplishments of American musicians are truly astounding. There are many extant works in the current literature that exploit their skill. In the *Sonata for Tuba and Piano* I have tried to utilize both the technical and the musicianship aspects of both players in the hope that the piece will be convincing to the listener.

The first movement derives its energy in part from the use of ostinato, occasional meter changes, and a limited use of asymmetry. A brief moment of relaxation occurs before the final drive to the end. Throughout the movement there is constant and very tight interplay between the two parts. The second movement explores various pedal points in the piano and some aleatory writing for the tuba. Dotted rhythms in Lombard style are quite evident. The third movement is a short, fast, scherzo-like piece with a prolonged keyboard ostinato supporting a rhythmic melodic line in the tuba as a middle section. The fourth movement introduces some new material, but it borrows heavily from the material of the previous three movements. The motion is furious, and it is rhythmically difficult.

I would like to make two observations about the piece. First, the metronome indications in the fast movements should be considered the minimum, and higher speeds are encouraged, with the caveat that clarity must be preserved at all times. Second, I have, for many years, included in most of my compositions a type of musical signature. This work is no exception and it shows up in all the movements.

Richard Peaslee (b. 1930)

Richard Peaslee was educated at Yale University and the Juilliard School and has studied composition with Nadia Boulanger and William Russo. He has written scores for the Royal Shakespeare Company, The National Theatre in London,

The New York Shapespeare Festival, and Broadway and off-Broadway shows. His concert works include *Animal Farm*, *The Marat/Sade Music*, *The Garden of Earthly Delights*, and *Vienna Lusthaus*.

The Devil's Herald

Hackensack, NJ: Helicon Music, Inc., 1975.
Movements: Sectional: Declamatory—Driving—Much Slower —Brighter—Tempo Primo
Instrumentation: Solo Tuba, four Horns, and Percussion (two players)

The Devil's Herald was composed for Harvey Phillips in 1975 and received its first performance in New York's Carnegie Recital Hall.

Not having written a solo piece for tuba before, I tried to come up with a concept of the instrument other than the traditional one of bass to the brass section of the orchestra. Conceiving of the tuba as a sort of massive prehistoric trumpet seemed to help trigger ideas for the work. In the opening fanfare section, the French horns prepare the way for a herald-like solo on the tuba. Percussion is used to give a primitive drive to the next portion of the piece; and in the third section, the lyric aspect of the tuba is displayed against the pulsating and undulating accompaniment from the horns. Effects such as glissandi, flutter tongue, and wind sounds through the instruments are used to create a mysterious atmosphere in the next part. There is then a return to the energetic, declamatory mood of the opening in the final two sections of the piece.

Vincent Persichetti (1915–1987)

Parable for Solo Tuba (Parable XXII) Op. 147

Bryn Mawr, PA: Elkan-Vogel, Inc., 1983.
Movements: One Movement, sectional
Instrumentation: Tuba alone

The *Parable for Solo Tuba* was commissioned by and dedicated to Harvey Phillips in 1981 and premiered by him at Carnegie Recital Hall in New York City on April 25, 1982. Along with the *Serenade No. 12*, also for solo tuba, these two compositions represent the only solo works written for tuba by Persichetti.

The parable series is an extensive collection of more than two dozen works, all containing the word "parable," for many different media. Eleven are for solo wind instruments; six are for solo string instruments, including piano and harpsichord; one is a two-act opera; and the remaining *Parables* are for carillon, organ, piano trio, string quartet, brass quintet, and band. The *Parable for Solo Tuba* is the last of the wind *Parables*.

All the *Parables* contain material from previous compositions by Persichetti. In a letter to the writer dated March 5, 1985, Persichetti stated: "Parables are musical essays that convey a meaning indirectly by the use of comparisons or analogies." The *Parable for Solo Tuba* is no exception, as portions of *The Creation* (1970) for vocal quartet, mixed chorus, and orchestra are used to generate similar melodic shapes and rhythmic proportions in this work.

In the same letter, Persichetti explored the relationship of *The Creation* to the *Parable for Solo Tuba*: "Think of a tuba player backstage during intermission improvising on a basic segment of *The Creation* having just been performed. Think of the composer (me) shaping the fragments that the original fragment begat into a musical form that stands on its own."

Out of the 160 measures of the *Parable for Solo Tuba*, the writer was able to discern *Creation* fragments for the first 67 measures. Only one section, measures 77–101, appears to have been composed of entirely new material. Much of the material modified from *The Creation* can be associated with the text present in the original, and thus invites extramusical associations. A complete analysis of this relationship is beyond the scope of these program notes but interested scholars may refer to the writer's "The Brass Parables of Vincent Persichetti," a DMA dissertation completed in 1985 at Arizona State University. Suffice it to say that the majority of the identifiable excerpts use the words "darkness," "silence," and "secret" in the context of the void prior to creation in the biblical sense. The rest of the *Parable* contains material stated previously but in a modified way. The formal scheme of the *Parable for Solo Tuba* can be outlined as follows:

Section:	A	B	C	D	E	F
Measures:	1–16	17–23	24–51	52–63	64–76	77–101

A'	B'	B''	A''	B'''	F'	A'''
102–11	112–29	130–32	133–38	139–51	152–55	158–60

As one can see, Persichetti is interested primarily in the small-section approach. It is interesting to note that melodic and rhythmic material returns, but never in its original form. Persichetti accomplishes this phenomenon through two compositional devices termed "autogenesis" and "interversion." The former describes a process of "constant repetition at the expense of literal repetition" (Robert Evett, *Juilliard Review* 2/3 [1955]:19). The latter was coined by Rudolph Reti and means "interchanging the notes of a thematic shape in order to produce a new one" (*The Thematic Process of Music*, 1951).

Parable for Solo Tuba is one of the most difficult contemporary solo tuba works that does not rely on avant-garde techniques. The range is extensive, from DD below the bass staff to A three ledger lines and a space above the bass staff. Its characteristic range is in the upper part of the staff and above it; this, coupled with a performance time of 13' 30", can lead to severe endurance problems. The rhythms are quite complex, although they are written within standard time signatures and ordinary note configurations. The rhythm configurations often use sixteenth and 32nd notes in a gestural capacity linking two or more motivic "cells." One of the most unusual aspects of the *Parable* is that tempo and dynamic changes occur every few bars. Just for statistical comparison, in this 160-measure composition, there are 36 tempo changes, 42 time signature changes, and 138 changes of dynamic level. It is obvious from a cursory glance at the score that it is heavily edited by the composer, and every performance detail seems to be marked with some kind of device, be it note lengths, styles, tempi, or dynamics.

Although the score is fraught with extensive detail, complex rhythmic, motivic, and melodic ideas, and a large range, it is a finely crafted piece. It does demand a very accomplished tubist to make it work.

Program note by Mark Nelson, Associate Professor of Music at Millikin University in Decatur, IL.

Serenade No. 12 for Solo Tuba, Op. 88

Bryn Mawr, PA: Elkan-Vogel, Inc., 1963.
Movements: I. Intrada
             II. Arietta
            III. Mascherata
             IV. Capriccio
              V. Intermezzo
             VI. Marcia
Instrumentation: Tuba alone

Commissioned by Harvey Phillips, the *Serenade No. 12 for Solo Tuba* of Vincent Persichetti is one of the earlier "major works" for the tuba. It is cast in six concise movements and utilizes gestures, rhythmic devices, and intervallic materials stylistically similar to other well-known Persichetti works of the same period, including the *Symphony No. 6*, for band.

Persichetti wrote fifteen *Serenades* for a variety of media, and in notes for an interview wrote: "My *Serenades* are suites of love pieces, usually of the night. I would be shocked if I did not see more love pieces in my future." Persichetti was a tubist himself in his younger days, and his familiarity with the instrument undoubtedly contributed to the success with which these sentiments are conveyed in the *Serenade for Solo Tuba*. Though the six movements encompass a wide variety of moods, a feeling of fond humor and love underlies the entire work.

The first movement, "Intrada," is based on seconds, minor thirds, and perfect fourths. It begins with an introspective three-bar introduction, which gives way quite unexpectedly to a fast 4/4 for the remainder of the movement. This surprising turn of events so near the opening sets the gently humorous tone of the movement. The vigorous, syncopated materials which follow are interrupted several times by a motive marked *forte*, consisting of a large leap (a seventh or a tenth) upward and four descending eighth notes like a shout of playful laughter. The composer regularly inserts unexpected dynamic changes throughout the movement, creating light-hearted suspense until the final *piano* descending major seventh.

The second movement, "Arietta," in 9/8, consists of three varied statements of a flowing seven-bar melody.

"Mascherata," the third movement, is marked "giocoso, ma con grazia." Groves describes the word "Mascherata" as relating to "masquerade" and further states that it is "A type of Villanella probably intended to be sung or played by street players. . . . They often included some element of caricature of a person or type. . . ." The melody of the "Mascherata" is reminiscent of a folk dance, with its thirds and repeated sixteenth notes. Twice this melody becomes more syncopated and agitated, following the marking "poco cresc. ed accel.," only to turn sentimental and slow again. A brief transitional section ("calmato") leads to a coda in which the opening motive becomes ever softer and slower.

The fourth movement, "Capriccio," makes the most demands on the player's technique and agility. The movement is in a fairly fast duple meter, with a half note equal to 96. The primary materials are alternating bars of triplet runs followed by jagged eighth-note duplets. Interjections of descending sevenths and ninths reminiscent of the first movement complete these materials.

The fifth movement, "Intermezzo," is a simple "Adagietto" in an ABA form.

The sixth and boisterous final movement, "Marcia," is assembled from short motives which satirize many traditional march materials. Though most of these melodic fragments are bombastic, Persichetti succeeds in infusing them with humor and gentle satire.

When one considers how few "role models" for tuba pieces existed when this work was written, it is a testament to the genius of Persichetti that he chose an overall tone of warm fondness and playfulness, very different from the easy stereotypes for such a work, and that he communicated these feelings with such success throughout.

Because the technical demands of the movements of the *Serenade* vary greatly, it is worthwhile to mention an editor's note that *Serenade No. 12* may be used as both a concert and a study piece. Students may use "Arietta," "Mascherata," and "Intermezzo" as preparatory studies for the more difficult "Intrada," "Capriccio," and "Marcia."

Program note by Jay Krush, who is a composer and a founding member and tubist of the Chestnut Brass Company.

Morgan Powell (b. 1938)

Morgan E. Powell is Professor of Music Composition at the University of Illinois, Urbana.

Midnight Realities

Nashville, TN: Brass Press, 1972.
Movements: One continuous movement
Instrumentation: Tuba alone

Midnight Realities was composed in 1972 for my dear friend Dan Perantoni. The work has been performed throughout the U.S.A. and Europe by Perantoni and others. It is sometimes performed together with *Transitions* for solo tuba and instrumental ensemble. The piece explores the wide range of technical/expressive potential of the tuba. The title refers to those quiet isolated hours of the night when ideas suddenly come to consciousness in intelligent forms.

Midnight Realities has been recorded on Crystal Recordings, together with *Transitions*, as a suite entitled *Nocturnes*, by Dan Perantoni and the University of Illinois Contemporary Chamber Players.

William Presser (b. 1916)

William Presser is Professor Emeritus of Music at the University of Southern Mississippi at Hattiesburg.

Capriccio for Tuba and Band

Bryn Mawr, PA: Tenuto Publications, 1970.
Movements: Allegro
Instrumentation: Tuba and Band

Written for Rex Conner. A rondo, 2/4, B♭ tonality. Full score is in C, nontransposing. One fast tempo throughout. I made rhythmic contrast by writing sections in longer note values. More fanfare-like passages than usual for me. A show-off piece for the tuba, lightly scored. 5 1/2 minutes. More harmonic passages than in most of my writing, no tricky rhythms. There is a measured cadenza for the tuba near the end of the work. College level for band, college-professional level for tuba.

Concerto for Tuba and Strings

Bryn Mawr, PA: Tenuto Publications, 1971.
Movements: I. Allegro
                        II. Allegro
                        III. Allegro molto
Instrumentation: Tuba and String Orchestra

Piano reduction and tuba part for sale. String parts on rental. Since I played violin and viola, the string writing is idiomatic. No key signatures are used.

Movement I: "Allegro." 4/4, D minor. The main theme has two ideas, one lyric, starting with a string unison, and one rhythmic. At the end of the development, a long, rhythmic ostinato in 5/4 occurs in the basses, with the tuba warming up the main theme for the recapitulation. A brief coda uses the lyric theme at a slower tempo. 7' 28".

Movement II: "Allegro." 3/4, D minor. Waltz-scherzo, with a slower middle section, and D.S., but no trio. 4' 22".

Movement III: "Allegro molto," 4/4, D minor. A rondo, with a 3/4 section in the middle. 4' 40".

While there is no slow movement, there are slow sections. College-professional level for strings and tuba.

Sonatina for Tuba and Piano

Bryn Mawr, PA: Tenuto Publications, 1973.
Movements: I. Allegretto
                        II. Allegro
                        III. Adagio
                        IV. Presto
Instrumentation: Tuba and Piano

Movement I: 4/4, C major. An alternation of two themes, lyric (A) and rhythmic (B). Each return of a theme is a development of that theme. Measure 1 = A, m. 21 = B, m. 40 = A, m. 49 = B (but it sounds like a new theme at first), m. 66 = A, m.

74 = cadenza on A and B, m. 95 = B, mm. 110–22 = A, slower tempo than at first. 4' 50".

Movement II: "Allegro," 3/4, D minor. The tempo of quarter note = 126 is too slow to call it a scherzo. It is more marchlike. Some oom-pa but a lot of counterpoint. 3' 30".

Movement III: "Adagio," 3/4, C minor. Sometimes to get a theme I think of a phrase like "Praise ye the Almighty" or "Horses are animals," but here I use a poem by Robert Herrick, "Another Grace for a Child." The music fits the whole poem, which starts: "Here a little child I stand, /Heaving up my either hand." The text is printed under the notes it fits, but it is not meant to be sung. The entire movement is a two-voice canon, with the piano following at an octave or two higher or lower. The only writing of more than two voices is the Amen. 1' 8".

Movement IV: "Presto," 4/4, E minor to C major. Actually in cut time, to be played as fast as possible. The tuba has four half notes; about twenty quarters, not counting notes at ends of phrases, which sound shorter; and the rest, about 560 quarter notes. The third from the last measure, all eighth notes, may be played several times to enhance the perpetual motion effect. 1'.

Second Sonatina for Tuba and Piano

Bryn Mawr, PA: Tenuto Publications, 1974.
Movements: I. Allegretto
              II. Adagio
            III. Allegro
Instrumentation: Tuba and Piano

This is a rather quiet work, with each movement beginning and ending softly, and not a lot of loud passages in between.

Movement I: "Allegretto," 3/4, G minor. Main theme is in three-voice counterpoint. Four loud chords introduce the sub-theme, with the tuba playing a more rhythmic tune than the main theme, and accompanied by 25 low fifths in the piano, then back to mostly three-voice counterpoint. The development is mostly that of the second theme, which ends with a measured cadenza in the tuba. There are two beats of *fortissimo* in this movement. 3' 52".

Movement II: "Adagio," 4/4, C minor. One four-measure theme, which occurs five times with a few interludes in between.

Movement III: "Allegro," 6/8, G major. If the metronome marking is quarter note = 120, it should be dotted quarter=120. The main theme is an eight-bar lilting theme which does not sound fast, and is expanded to eleven bars. The tuba alone has it first, then the piano, then tuba with piano accompaniment. The second theme is a noisy one, sounding like the first part of the nursery rhyme "Baa, Baa, black sheep, have you any. . . ." That's as far as the resemblance goes. This section ends with two measures of *fortissimo*. The main theme returns with a little crossing of 2/4 and 6/8 between the tuba and piano. The rude "Baa Baa" returns briefly, and a short coda has a few loud downward scales taken from the end of the main theme, plus a *pianissimo* ending, which does not slow down. There are few ritards in my music. When I want them I mark them. There are three measures of *fortissimi*. 1' 44".

Suite for Tuba

Buffalo, NY: Ensemble Publications, 1967.
Movements: I. Allegretto
                        II. Adagio—Allegro
                        III. Adagio—Allegro
Instrumentation: Tuba alone

This work was written for Rex Conner in August 1966. The first movement, marked "Allegretto," is in 4/4 time with four flats in the signature and a tonality of B♭, with a hint of Dorian mode. It is marchlike in style. The second movement, marked "Adagio—Allegro," opens slowly in 4/4 time with three flats in the signature; it is followed by a 6/8 *allegro*, also marchlike. The third movement, also marked "Adagio—Allegro," is in 4/4 time with four flats in the signature, again with B♭ as the tonality hinting at the Dorian mode. This movement is also marchlike, but faster. A college-level piece.

David Reck (b. 1935)

David Reck is Professor of Music and of Asian Languages and
Civilizations at Amherst College, Amherst, MA.

Five Studies for Tuba Alone

New York: C. F. Peters, 1968.
Movements: I. Tempo Rubato
             II. As fast as possible, with clarity
             III. Like a song
             IV. Make like a Wallenda, man!
             V. Blues
Instrumentation: Tuba alone

Dedicated to Harvey Phillips, *Five Studies for Tuba Alone* was
written in the fabled days of the 1960s, when innovation,
experimentation, creative imagination, freedom, and a touch
of whimsy were in the ascendant. In those *Sgt. Pepper* times,
frigid minimalism and modish post-modernism had not yet
raised their retrogradable heads, and the wizardry of electronics and synthesizers had not yet made music composition
child's play to any reasonably intelligent five-year-old.
    I had met Harvey in 1966, when he was busily trying to
convince everybody that the tuba was an underutilized instrument capable of doing much more than was ever written for
it; in short, the tuba was a swan which had been stereotyped
as an ugly duckling or, more correctly, a rumbling rhino! I
asked him to sit down with me and show me all the tricks
which he, as a marvelous virtuoso, had in his incredible grab-
bag. I then set about trying to incorporate these elements into
a series of brief pieces.
    The five studies are all unmetered, although the second is
metrical in a sense, and all give considerable freedom to the
performer in choosing the details of rhythm and duration as
well as interpretation. Though the pieces may seem to the
casual listener to be twelve-tone or atonal, they were com-

posed by ear and intuition. I was at the time (and still am) influenced by the painters of abstract expressionism (Jackson Pollack, especially), and I tried to create music in a process of "automatic handwriting" without too much interference from the rational/formal part of the brain. (Looking back on the pieces after more than twenty years, I can observe the importance of strings of three-note-groups consisting of a third and a major seventh or minor ninth; the tritone; and the gravitational pull of certain tonal poles.)

Movement I: The opening study ("Tempo rubato") is a kind of expressionist recitative with gentle melodic gestures contrasting with sudden and almost violent outbursts.

Movement II: The second ("As fast as possible, with clarity") is a series of fast eighth-note constellations separated by "pockets" of silence. This study also represents a composer's miscalculation; tuba players can play faster than I imagined, so the metronomic marking of quarter note = 136 is closer to my intention.

Movement III: The third study ("Like a song") is an arabesque.

Movement IV: The title of the fourth study ("Make like a Wallenda, man!") comes from an image in my mind's eye that likens the virtuosity and skill of a musician with that of a circus performer. In this case the reference is to the greatest high-wire act in circus history, the Wallenda Family. On January 30, 1962 in Detroit something went wrong as they were walking across a high wire without a net in their unprecedented seven-person pyramid, and two fell to their deaths. The next night the survivors were back up on the wire. This movement has its share of virtuosic tricks and balancing acts: singing and playing simultaneously, flutter tongues, trills, and so on.

Movement V: The final study ("Blues") begins with a lip glissando, a wild animal call, and huge stalking footsteps. I like to think of a dinosaur in a prehistoric fern jungle. (Remember, in the 60s these extinct creatures had not yet become cute and cuddly things for the under-seven set.) More lyric passages follow (an animalistic lament, or agony), and the leviathan stalks off with one more cry.

Kjell Roikjer (b. 1901)

Sonata for Tuba and Piano, Op. 68

Copenhagen: Imudico A/S, 1981.
Movements: I. Allegro moderato e energico
             II. Molto lento e pesante
            III. Allegro energico e een agevolezza
Instrumentation: Tuba and Piano

The *Sonata for Tuba and Piano*, Op. 68, was written in 1976 for my young friend and colleague, solo tubist in the Stockholm Philharmonic Orchestra, Michael Lind. I have known Mr. Lind since 1974, when he premiered my *Tuba Concerto*. Since then we have been in continuous contact, which has resulted in some twenty works for solo tuba as well as chamber music for brass, including *Capriccio for Tuba and Orchestra* (1974); *Practice Pieces for Tuba and Piano* in all keys; thirty *Inventions* for two, three, and four tubas; and fifteen chamber works for various combinations of brass instruments.

Movement I: F major. Begins with a distinct rhythmically tense theme. Through a closely related second theme of a milder character, it moves on to a calmer theme in B minor. A dreamlike mood develops over a climax (*pesante*), after which the opening theme returns.

Movement II: A heavy, somewhat melancholy section in D minor in 6/4 is followed by a short bell motive. The initial motive returns and the music gradually fades away.

Movement III: Also in F major and written as a scherzo in a light *duo concertante* form. The introduction and ending are based on a short distinct motive. A race develops between the two instruments, but is interrupted by a somewhat milder imaginative middle section, after which the piece resolves.

Translated by Michael Lind.

Walter Ross (b. 1936)

Walter Ross is Professor of Composition at the University of
Virginia at Charlottesville.

Concerto for Tuba and Band

New York: Boosey and Hawkes, 1975.
Movements: I.   Overture (Allegro vivo)
                II. Berceuse (Calm)
                III. Toccata (Adagio—Allegro)
Instrumentation: Tuba and Band

My *Tuba Concerto* was requested by and is dedicated to R.
Winston Morris, who premiered the work brilliantly at the
University of Virginia in the Spring of 1973. As a brass performer myself, I knew there were only a few works which
featured the tuba as a solo instrument, and many of them fit
the "cute" category. I decided to write a concerto for tuba and
band that was serious, two-fisted, and no-nonsense: something
that did not present the tuba in a comic manner, that would
make the audience sit up and think of the tuba as a major solo
instrument.

The *Tuba Concerto* is thirteen minutes in length and written in three movements, each in ABA form. The first
movement, entitled "Overture," is energetic, and might be described as a series of fanfares and interludes. The second
movement, "Berceuse," is a cradle song. The quiet, rocking
accompaniment in the ensemble at the opening of this movement sets the relaxed mood. The middle section has a slightly
faster motion, with the saxophone quartet in dialogue with
the solo tuba. After a short introduction, the last movement
returns to the energy level of the first, altered only by a brief,
slower B section. Throughout the concerto, the percussion
section plays an important role behind the solo, providing
rhythmic and coloristic accompanimental patterns. In fact,

the percussion group forms a third contrasting unit to the solo tuba and the concert band, making the *Tuba Concerto* different from the traditional concerto, which contrasts only two instrumental units—the solo instrument and the ensemble.

The work is intended to display the virtuosic ability of the tuba soloist, but the band parts are of a difficulty suitable for a good collegiate concert band. No unusual instruments are required beyond what would be available to any full band.

The *Tuba Concerto* is available for both full band and tuba solo, and piano reduction and tuba solo.

Midnight Variations

Medfield, MA: Dorn Publications, Inc., 1971.
Movements: One movement, sectional
Instrumentation: Tuba and Prepared Tape

The main idea of *Midnight Variations* is to present the evolution of tuba technique in an impressionistic way. This seven-minute piece for solo tuba and tape is a miniature tone poem in that it is based on an extramusical idea: I present the tuba as a personality—as live, human music in opposition to the mechanical music on the tape. The title is a rather fanciful one. The word "variations" in this instance does not refer to a theme or melody which undergoes variations. Instead, as the work unfolds, the listener hears an evolution of tuba technique.

At the beginning, there are mysterious, primeval sounds on the tape, which the tuba imitates—not being yet a tuba. The tape then makes a tuba-like sound, which the tuba also imitates. The interval expands from a unison to "the perfect bass-line interval." As the tuba practices this interval, the tape slowly fades into ragtime, which the tuba accompanies. The tuba soon abandons this imitative role, however, and takes off in another direction—the tape now accompanying the tuba with a "side-man" effect. The tuba becomes more and more virtuosic, eventually overwhelming even the tape. This virtuosity ends with "explosions" on the tape, and both, overcome by their exertions, fall back to the primeval sounds of the beginning.

Midnight Variations was written at the request of Barton
Cummings while he was in Vietnam with a service band. At
that time I had not yet met him. He was a friend of one of my
students, who was also serving in Vietnam and who had mentioned to him that I liked to write for brass. Cummings
premiered the work, and later I wrote *Piltdown Fragments* (tuba
and tape) for him, which he premiered at Carnegie Recital Hall
in New York.

Charles Ruggiero (b. 1947)

Charles Ruggiero is Professor of Composition and Music Theory
and Co-director of the Computer Music Studio at Michi-
gan State University, East Lansing.

Fractured Mambos

East Lansing, MI: Charles Ruggiero, 1990.
Movements: One movement, sectional
Instrumentation: Tuba and Electronic Tape

Early in 1989 Philip Sinder asked me if I would be interested
in writing a piece for tuba. I offered to write one for solo tuba
and electronic tape with a strong jazz flavor. Phil, who shares
my interest in jazz, had been considering the same combination of performing forces, so it was easy for us to agree on the
broad outlines of the collaboration which has resulted in
Fractured Mambos.

While writing for tuba, and while preparing to write by listening to diverse recorded examples of tuba music, I was
impressed by the wide range of sounds, moods, and emotions
that this beast of an instrument is able to convey when tamed
by a performer as masterful as Philip Sinder. The tuba, I found,
can be clumsy, comical, playful, lyrical, bold, dramatic. It can

be delicately expressive one second and magnificently intimidating the next.

Instead of using real-time electronic modification of tuba sounds, I decided to use a "classical" technique in this work, combining prerecorded synthesized and digitally sampled sounds with the live, unprocessed tuba performance. I took this approach because I did not wish to turn the tuba into some sort of electric trumpet or *MIDI* wind controller; I wanted it to produce natural timbres and articulations. It was my intention to create a work that would be relatively easy to perform "on the road," with minimal hardware requirements and a simple setup. Furthermore, I did not want my new composition to become outdated as soon as the current generation of computer music hardware was replaced by the next wave of technology.

A concept of the timbres and textures to be used in *Fractured Mambos* came to me soon after I decided to write the piece. At first there were to be four main sound groups: the live acoustic tuba part, digitally sampled brass ensemble sounds, synthesized and sampled percussion sounds, and synthesized tuba sounds. Later, a fifth sound group was added: sampled muted trumpet/tuba sounds.

The textural and timbral models for *Fractured Mambos* should be familiar to many listeners. They include post-bop big bands (with their powerful trumpet and trombone sections) and Latin/jazz salsa groups (which typically combine horns with dynamic four-to-six-member rhythm sections).

Eclectic in style, *Fractured Mambos* clearly shows the influence on my work of such leading twentieth-century American musicians as Thelonious Monk, Gil Evans, and Miles Davis. Echoes (that are sometimes twisted and distorted but are never intentionally mocking) of the music of such Latin/jazz artists as Tito Puente and Chick Corea are pervasive in *Fractured Mambos*. What may be its main structural premise—the transformation, reinterpretation, and disintegration of somewhat simple and "familiar" musical materials through juxtaposition, interruption, and interpolation—comes in no small part from that ancient and esteemed master I.S.

Armand Russell (b. 1932)

Armand Russell is Professor of Music at the University of Hawaii at Honolulu.

Suite Concertante for Tuba and Woodwind Quintet

Athens, OH: Accura Music, 1963.
Movements: I. Capriccio
                      II. Ballade
                     III. Scherzo
                      IV. Burlesca
Instrumentation: Tuba and Woodwind Quintet

Suite Concertante for Tuba and Woodwind Quintet was written for Roger Bobo; the initial idea arose when we both were playing in the Rochester Philharmonic and Civic orchestras in 1958. The preliminary version was with a piano accompaniment, and the first performance by Roger was of this version. The final version, with woodwind quintet, followed very soon, and in this form Roger Bobo gave the premiere in 1961.

At that time there were many fewer solos for tuba, and there was relatively little variety in the use of chamber ensembles with a tuba solo, something that has changed markedly in the interim. The choice of this instrumentation came from my desire for color contrast and diversity that would help create a festive, emotionally varied piece.

The work is organized in four movements with rather Classic formal relationships between the movements: fast, slow, scherzo, fast. The style is largely neoclassic but with little emotional restraint. The tuba is certainly prominent, and it plays a more important role than any of the other instruments. However, it is not a display function, as it might have in a concerto. While the tuba is the most prominent voice, the other instruments periodically surface in modest solo roles rather than function as a consistently antiphonal or adversarial body.

The first movement uses a sonata allegro form. Although its mood is suggested by the title, "Capriccio," it also includes a degree of seriousness. The tuba states the first theme, which emphasizes half steps and minor thirds. The woodwinds come to the fore in the transition. The tuba then returns with the second theme, which is based on skips of an octave, a seventh, and sixths in a lyric setting. The energetic and active development section begins with a prominent moment for the horn, followed by the oboe presenting the first theme, now set in compound time. Fragments of the theme presage the answering of the tuba, and soon portions of the second theme enter into the process. After a critical clash between tuba and bassoon in the lower register, the recapitulation begins, thereby bringing some stability yet reinstating the earlier motility and spirit. Again the tuba carries the first theme, but moves it to a new pitch level. A brief reappearance of the second theme is also stated by the tuba. It leads to the Coda, where the woodwinds present portions of their original accompaniment for the first theme to round out the movement with a gentle mood.

The second movement, "Ballade," includes a singing style in a slow tempo. The form is ternary, ABA'. Section A is itself a little ternary; the tuba presents the principal theme, with its small skips and stepwise motion, both before and after a middle section featuring the flute and bassoon. Section B employs larger skips with arpeggio-like figures, and it has a lyric approach. The tuba returns to section A, after which a very brief Coda uses woodwind motives over a pedal in the tuba.

Ternary form is also used in the "Scherzo," the third movement. The opening figure in the tuba covers a range of two octaves in two measures. Its brashness is answered by the woodwinds. A fragmentary texture creates a bantering context in which colors shift rapidly. The brief trio section features a singing line in the tuba, doubled by the horn two octaves above. The returning first section is also very brief and brings back the mix of tuba and woodwind colors and a fragmented texture to close the movement.

Rondo form is used in the last movement, "Burlesca." A five-note motive is prominent in the primary theme and is reminiscent of the first movement, but here tritones are emphasized and lend a sinister undertone to the proceedings, capricious though they seem at times. In the form ABA'CA" Coda, the tuba is prominent in the first four sections. Sections B and C bring out the lyric qualities of the tuba in contrast to the more intense forward motion of the principal sections. The last statement of section A features the flute and the oboe. It is followed by the Coda, which has a faster tempo and rapid flurries of celebrative scale figures in the tuba.

Ole Schmidt (b. 1928)

Concerto for Tuba and Orchestra

Copenhagen: Edition Wilhelm Hansen, 1977.
Movements: I. Quarter note = 100
               II. Quarter note = 50
               III. Allegro, Quarter note = 126
Instrumentation: Tuba and Orchestra

The first performance of my tuba concerto took place in Copenhagen on November 17, 1976, played by Michael Lind, to whom it is dedicated. I had the pleasure of accompanying Michael by conducting the Copenhagen Philharmonic.

The work has three movements: Allegro moderato, Lento, Allegro guisto. The total length is 14' 20".

The scoring is for two flutes, two oboes, two clarinets, two bassoons, four French horns, timpani, two percussionists, eight violas, and four double basses. No violins are involved. My wish was to build the piece on "darker" colors. However, the high registers are covered by the woodwinds. The concerto was made in close collaboration with Michael Lind. He demonstrated for me in the most convincing way, what a contemporary tuba player can do on his instrument.

The concerto was recorded by Edition Wilhelm Hansen LPWH 111 on November 1, 1979 in Aarhus, with Michael Lind and the Aarhus Symphony Orchestra, conducted by me.

William Schmidt (b. 1926)

William Schmidt is President of Western International Music, Inc., in Greeley, CO.

Concertino for Tuba and Woodwind Quintet

Los Angeles: Avant Music, 1980. Sole selling agent: Western International Music, Inc., Greeley, CO.
Movements: I. Half note = 120
               II. Quarter note = 69
               III. Half note = 126
Instrumentation: Tuba and Woodwind Quintet

The *Concertino for Tuba and Woodwind Quintet* was actually written for bass trombonist Terry Cravens, Professor of Trombone at the University of Southern California. The tuba version was considered at the time of composition because of the proximity in range of the two instruments. Thus what was written as a difficult trombone piece was also a not-so-difficult tuba piece. The work is in a three-movement conventional form, i.e., fast—slow—fast, and it utilizes the colors of the woodwinds to enhance the solo line. The *Concertino* is rather light in character and is most accessible to university-level players.

Serenade for Tuba and Piano

Greeley, CO: Western International Music, Inc., 1962.
Movements: I. Romanza
               II. Waltz
               III. Dirge
               IV. March
Instrumentation: Tuba and Piano

The *Serenade* was written for Tommy Johnson when he and I

were fellow students at the University of Southern California. The original version, written in 1958, had seven movements, but it was reduced to four at the time of its premiere by Mr. Johnson for my Master's recital in 1960. This work has been recorded by Rex Conner on Coronet Records and by Tommy Johnson on WIM Records. The following review and analysis by Mary Rasmussen in the Spring 1963 issue of *Brass Quarterly* is the most eloquent statement about the work that has been made:

> William Schmidt's *Serenade* is an extremely well worked-out piece, although the movements are very short. The first movement, "Romanza," is slow, with expressive chromatic intervals which have a habit of doubling back or inverting upon themselves a half step higher or lower; and a pliable, spun-out melodic line with a snatch of canon in the middle. The dissonant, chromatic-quartal harmonies are effectively arranged. The almost atonal "Waltz" is cleverly put together with canon, inverted canon, and a great deal of wit. The "Dirge" is a colorful, darting, thrusting, yet somber movement with a rolling rhythm. The "March" is chromatic, pointillistic, and very humorous. The whole work is extremely imaginative and varied—by far the most interesting of the short pieces published for tuba and piano—with care and craft put into it such as one rarely encounters in music for these instruments.

Sonata for Tuba and Piano

Greeley, CO: Western International Music, Inc., 1984.
Movements: I. Moderately
                II. Slowly
                III. Moderately fast
Instrumentation: Tuba and Piano

The *Sonata for Tuba and Piano* was commissioned by and written for Mel Culbertson, who premiered it with Chantal de Buchy, piano, at the Paris Conservatory of Music in 1982. Final revisions were made in 1983, and it was published in 1984.

The first movement begins with muted tuba playing the main

theme in canon with the piano. After a short, slower interlude, the mood changes to a quicker tempo and a contrasting theme. This secondary theme develops into the main musical activity of the movement and includes an alternating and less-active development of the main theme. The last utterances of the secondary theme lead back to a slow Coda and ending.

The second movement is a rondo. The A section is slow and moody, followed by a fast sixteenth-note B section. The A^1 part returns as a ritornello, slightly developed, leading into the B^1 part, another fast sixteenth-note section. The movement ends with the A^2 ritornello, moody and slow.

The third movement starts marchlike, with the piano and tuba in unison. As the piano breaks off to continue the rhythmic motive, the tuba introduces a leaping motive. This grows into a lyrical ABA transition, followed by a large developed section dominated by a pushing motor rhythm. The ending is a return to the marching theme taken from the introduction.

Tony and the Elephant or Jim and the Roadrunner

Los Angeles: Avant Music, 1984. Sole selling agent: Western International Music, Inc., Greeley, CO.
Movements: I. Stomp'n'
             II. Waltz'n'
             III. Blues'n'
             IV. Swing'n'
             V. Trip'n'
Instrumentation Tuba and C Trumpet

Tony and the Elephant or Jim and the Road Runner was written for Tony Plog, trumpet, and Jim Self, tuba, for a WIM Recording. A unique feature of this work is the use of matching mutes (cup, bucket, and straight) by the two instrumentalists. This is a jazz-inspired work with the following characteristics:

I. "Stomp'n'": In 2/2 time, this movement drives along with an insistent staccato quarter-note rhythm. (Open horns.)

II. "Waltz'n'": The 3/4 rhythm predominates in the tuba part, while the trumpet part contains figures of sixteenth notes in groups of six, and grace-note patterns. (Cup mutes.)

III. "Blues'n'": In 7/4—a slow moody conversation between two lines that interchange. Bending notes is required, as well as portamentos. (Bucket mutes.)

IV. "Swing'n'": In cut time, this movement has a traditional jazz style with plenty of syncopations and dotted eighth notes. (Straight mutes.)

V. "Trip'n'": The staccato quarter-note rhythm appears again, but cast in multiple time changes throughout, with a variety of melodic utterances. (Open horns.)

Tuba Mirum for Tuba, Winds and Percussion

Greeley, CO: Western International Music, Inc., 1984.
Movements: One movement, sectional
Instrumentation: Tuba, Winds, and Percussion

The *Tuba Mirum* was commissioned by and written for Michael Lind in 1983 and was published in 1984. It was premiered by Ron Davis at California State University, Fullerton, with Benton Minor conducting.

The theme is based on the Gregorian chant from the "Dies Irae" of the *Missae pro Defunctis*. The work opens with an ostinato in the harp, piano, and chimes accompanying the solo tuba playing the *Tuba Mirum* chant. This introduction builds with the addition of mallet percussion and eventually the entire wind ensemble.

A transition section leads into Variation I, which features the tuba and piccolo in duet with accompanying low brass. Variation II is calm and serene, with an ABA structure. The B section is busy, with its sixteenth-note passages, but then it returns to the long line eighth-note melody that characterized the opening serenity.

Variation III is almost an entire movement in itself. The use of jazz figures predominates throughout and helps "bind" together the several variants that make up this large variation. A dramatic Coda is eventually introduced and works itself into a quiet ending. The accompaniment closes the work in the same manner as it appeared in the opening introductory passages.

Tunes

Greeley, CO: Western International Music, Inc., 1990.
Movements: I. A Little Off
            II. A Little Under
           III. A Little Out
Instrumentation: Tuba and 23 Winds

Tunes was commissioned by T.U.B.A., under the sponsorship of the city of Sapporo, Japan, where it was premiered by James Self at the International Music Festival in August 1990.

Movement I: "A Little Off" is derived from my 1989 composition for tuba and percussion called *Latin Rhythms*. The rhythmic pattern in 5/8 utilizes false fingerings in the solo, saxophone, trumpet, and horn parts. By playing the fingerings instead of the notes, a sense of being "a little off" (out of tune) is achieved. A "little off" also connotes being a little crazy!

Movement II: "A Little Under" means a little "down" or "blue" (sad). Harmonies that accompany the solo originate from Gagako (traditional Japanese court music) played by the Sho (Japanese harmonica). This section is what I call Japanese blues. The movement is slow—fast—slow in form; after a middle section that is rhythmically punctuated, it returns to the Japanese blues.

Movement III: "A Little Out" is a sampling of "straight" music versus jazz. These two elements within the movement act as contrasts for the solo tuba, whose tune is a rhythmic and contrasting motive. This movement is a "little out," as opposed to "way out," but not quite "far out." It also "takes you out," or exits!

Gunther Schuller (b. 1925)

Gunther Schuller is a composer, a conductor, and an author. He is president of Margun Publishing Company, Newton Centre, MA.

Capriccio for Tuba and Orchestra

Movements: I. Slow—Allegro
                II. Adagio
                III. Molto adagio
Instrumentation: Tuba and Orchestra

My *Capriccio* was written in 1960 in response to the need in those early years for a serious literature for some of the "underdog" instruments of the orchestra, in this instance the tuba. More specifically it was written for (and is dedicated to) Harvey Phillips, who as a performer, a teacher, a commissioner of works for his instrument, and as a spokesman for the rights of the tuba has contributed more valiantly than anyone else I can think of. *Capriccio* was premiered in 1963 in Carnegie Recital Hall (now Weill Hall) on a pioneering series of contemporary music concerts that I initiated, called Twentieth Century Innovators, with Harvey Phillips as soloist, and me conducting.

In the program notes for the premiere concert, I wrote: "Though modest in intentions, the work is uncompromising in outlook, making no unnecessary concessions to the largely assumed or imagined limitations of the tuba. It presents the soloist with challenges which are musical as much as they are technical, and as such the *Capriccio* undoubtedly can look forward to a restful, undisturbed and unperformed future." This somewhat sombre prediction did not come true, for the work has had a fair number of performances over the last three decades.

The *Capriccio* is for tuba and chamber orchestra with a small string section of eight violins, three cellos, and two basses (no violas). It is in three movements, the first of which consists of a somewhat lyrical introduction, followed by an "Allegro" in which the tuba displays its agility in exchanging lively rhythmic patterns and melodic fragments with the orchestra.

The second movement is basically a variation movement. An opening statement is used as a sort of refrain which recurs several times throughout the movement in slightly altered forms, and which, in turn, leads the music in different directions, always returning eventually to the refrain idea.

The last movement, though brief, is set in a very slow tempo, almost suspended in time. The sustained elements in the strings serve as a backdrop against which reminiscences from the two previous movements are placed.

In general, I have tried to show that the tuba is not relegated to the few stereotypes associated with it and that, on the contrary, its range of expression, of colors, and of sonorities and its technical capacities are virtually unlimited.

Robert Sibbing (b. 1929)

Robert Sibbing is Professor of Music at Western Illinois University, at Macomb.

Sonata for Tuba and Piano

Bryn Mawr, PA: Tenuto Publications, 1970.
Movements: I. Allegro moderato
                II. Larghetto
               III. Allegro giocoso
Instrumentation: Tuba and Piano

The *Sonata for Tuba and Piano* was composed at the request of tubist Kent Campbell. The first movement was written in the summer of 1961, while I was studying with Robert Kelly at the

University of Illinois. The work was completed in early 1962, and the first performance took place shortly thereafter with Mr. Campbell, tuba, and Dean Boal, piano. It was next performed by Ron Bishop of the San Francisco Symphony. A recording by Daniel Perantoni, tuba, and Howard Karp, piano, was released later by University Brass Ensemble Series Records.

The piece was intended to display the lyrical and expressive capabilities of the tuba-and-piano combination. The first movement, marked "Allegro moderato," is cast in sonata allegro form, with a lighthearted first theme and a contemplative song for the second theme. The development features fugal procedures.

The second movement, "Larghetto," is a ternary form. Its somber mood is alleviated in the middle section, and the music ends with a feeling of resignation. The third and final movement, marked "Allegro giocoso," contrasts a jocular tune with themes of tenderness and buffoonery.

James Staples (b. 1934)

James Staples is Professor of Theory, Composition, and Piano at Indiana University of Pennsylvania, Indiana, PA.

Suite for Tuba and Piano

Indiana, PA: James Staples, 1989.
Movements: I. Allegro scherzando
              II. Adagio mesto
             III. Moderato con moto
              IV. Adagio espressivo
               V. Allegro vivace
Instrumentation: Tuba and Piano

The *Suite for Tuba and Piano* was written in the summer of

1989 at the request of Gary Bird, my colleague at Indiana University of Pennsylvania, and is dedicated to him. Gary wanted a new work to premiere on his solo program during that year's Octubafest. Since he and I had performed together on numerous occasions, I had a pretty good idea of the technical possibilities of the tuba and the sonic characteristics of the various registers. I was interested in portraying in each movement a decidedly different mood, carefully drawn in musical terms.

The opening "Allegro scherzando," as its name implies, is a capricious joke; but it involves some hazardous leaps from low register to high—at the outset, and several times thereafter. There is considerable imitation of this motive in the piano, and a contrasting *dolce* idea, which makes two brief appearances. The movement ends with a sardonic transfer from a sustained high F to a subterranean A.

The second movement features long-held notes involving slow *crescendos* and *diminuendos*—above the staff at the opening, and ending on four whole notes (*con sordino*) in the very lowest reaches. There is one quasi-cadenza passage for each instrument, played in the pervasively sad, mournful character of the entire movement. The pianist is required on occasion to use the sostenuto pedal, which will limit performances to instruments with a working middle pedal.

The "Moderato con moto" is the dance movement of the set. Here, a quixotic playfulness alternates with a beguiling, habanera-like rhythm. The tuba part introduces a motive containing a rapid, descending triplet figure, while the piano part contains many stretches of a ninth or a tenth with a moving line within. There is considerable musical interplay between the two.

The fourth movement is the lyrical focus of the suite. Its pop-ballad ambiance presents contours reminiscent of "My Old Flame" and "When You Wish upon a Star," while treating the solo instrument to some very sustained high notes as part of long lines. The pianist once again deals with sostenuto-pedal effects and large stretches. Dark, somber coloring characterizes both instruments at the close.

The "Finale" is a whimsical chase in sixteenth notes between the protagonists (the main motive employing rapid

finger work far easier on the piano than on the tuba!). As in
the first movement, a lyrical aside, *cantabile*, provides momentary relief from the general playfulness. The short codetta
finally has the piano making large, rapid leaps, while the tuba
belts out a descending arpeggio (*marcato*) of over two octaves.
The ending is, appropriately, abrupt and perfunctory.

Halsey Stevens (1908–1989)

Halsey Stevens was Professor Emeritus in the School of
Music, University of Southern California in Los Angeles.

Sonatina for Tuba or Trombone and Piano

New York: Peer-Southern Music Co., 1968.
Movements: I. Moderato con moto
                         II. Andante affettuoso
                         III. Allegro
Instrumentation: Tuba and Piano

In the spring of 1959 I was at Stetson University in Florida to
conduct the premiere performance of my *Testament of Life*,
commissioned in memory of Claude Almand, late Dean of the
Stetson School of Music. During my stay there I met Don
Waldrop, a fine tuba player, who asked me if I would consider
writing a work for him. Since I had somewhat earlier projected
a series of works which would cover all the standard orchestral
instruments, and was therefore attuned to the possibility, I in-
dicated interest. But when I returned to Stetson the following
autumn (to conduct the same work again), I had not found an
opportunity to write for tuba. However, at Don Waldrop's in-
sistence, I set to work when I returned home, and wrote the
Sonatina between November 11, 1959 and January 2, 1960.
Waldrop and Martine Sellars gave the first performance at

Stetson University on April 28, 1960.

When the work came to be published in 1968, in the process of editing I came to the realization that with a very few modifications it would become not only playable but idiomatic for the trombone as well. (It has been recorded in both versions: for tuba by Daniel Perantoni and Howard Karp, and on trombone by Donald Knaub and Barry Snyder.)

There are three relatively short movements; the entire duration is 9' 15". The first movement is marked by extreme rhythmic plasticity, although it is notated throughout in 3/4. There are two thematic groups, very slightly developed and varied in the recapitulation, with a Coda to round out the form. The "Andante" is expressive and lyrical, the "Allegro" brisk and brittle, dancelike in character, and a rondo in form (more or less ABA'B'A). Tonal allegiances: I and III, C; II, E.

(Program note written October 1, 1975; slightly revised May 25, 1978.)

John Stevens (b. 1951)

John D. Stevens is Associate Professor of Music at the University of Wisconsin-Madison, and a member of the Wisconsin Brass Quintet.

Dances

New York: Peer International Corporation, 1978.
Movements: One movement, sectional
Instrumentation: Tuba Solo with Tuba Trio Accompaniment

Dances was composed in 1975 and premiered by myself and three colleagues at my Masters recital at Yale University. It was later recorded by Toby Hanks and the other members of the New York Tuba Quartet (Steven Johns, Sam Pilafian, and myself) on Toby's *Sampler* album on Crystal Records. Since its publication *Dances* has become part of the standard repertoire for tubists all over the world.

Although *Dances* is one continuous piece, it is actually in three distinct sections, or movements, connected by improvised cadenzas in the solo part. There is a certain ethnic quality to the music, usually perceived as Spanish, and the melodies and harmonies are tonal and very traditional in nature. The shifting back and forth between minor and major modes is a unifying aspect of the piece.

The first movement (half note = 120), is light and bouncy, and is primarily in C minor, although a lowered second is used a great deal, giving the music the Spanish quality. This is followed by a cadenza in C minor that ends on a G. That leads to the second movement ("Slow," quarter note = 60), in the key of C major (with a shift to F major in the middle). This is a very expressive movement, made to sound somewhat free by the use of quintuplets and triplets in the solo part over the constant eighth-note arpeggiation in the accompaniment. The cadenza that follows is in C, but it uses a B♭ to create a dominant feel that leads to the third movement in the tonality of F, which was hinted at in the second movement. This movement is a fast 6/8 (dotted quarter = 144, though it is often played as fast as 160, even by the composer!) with the mode constantly changing from minor to major, with neither dominating. The ethnic flavor of the second and third movements is achieved largely through the consistent use of lowered sixth and seventh scale degrees.

The solo part of *Dances* works equally well on euphonium or bass tuba (E♭ or F). The three accompanying parts are in a range that can be played on any tuba.

Triumph of the Demon Gods

Cincinnati: Queen City Brass Publications, 1981.
Movements: One movement, sectional
Instrumentation: Tuba alone

Triumph of the Demon Gods was written in 1980 especially for an old friend, Michael Thornton, principal tubist with the Cincinnati Symphony. He premiered the work, and I later recorded it on my album, *Power* (Mark Records, No. 20699).

As usual in my music, there is something of a programmatic aspect to the work. The loud, low, "barbaric" section of the work (the "bad guys") is juxtaposed with the softer, higher, more melodic sections (the "good guys"). The two styles engage in musical battle throughout the piece, alternating constantly. The opening "barbaric" section returns at the end, but is marked "more barbaric." This, in addition to the title, indicates who prevails in the end.

Although the intention of this piece is to be fun for performer and listener alike, it is not a comic piece and can certainly be programmed in any recital situation.

The Liberation of Sisyphus

Madison, WI: John D. Stevens, 1990.
Movements: One movement
Instrumentation: Solo Tuba, Four Euphoniums, Four Tubas

The Liberation of Sisyphus was composed in the spring of 1990. It was commissioned by, and written especially for, world-renowned tuba virtuoso Roger Bobo. Roger commissioned the work for the 1990 International Tuba-Euphonium Conference in Sapporo, Japan, where the premiere was given with Roger as soloist and me conducting the Tokyo Bari-Tuba Ensemble as the accompanying group.

The title was conceived by Roger Bobo and was, in fact, an idea for a piece that he had had in mind for a long time. Mythology tells us that Sisyphus angered the gods and was condemned by Zeus to spend all eternity pushing a heavy stone up a hill. Roger was interested in a piece that would create its own mythology by representing the hypothetical liberation of Sisyphus. We collaborated on the basic shape of the work (within the bounds of a request for a six-to-eight-minute work for the conference), discussing the need to build up tremendous tension in the music that finally is relieved or resolved in a triumphant ending. The piece is programmatic in the sense that the general shape of the work represents the concept of the title.

As I began to compose the piece I realized that my two primary tasks were to create the proper mood of the piece in a relatively short time frame and to orchestrate it in such a way that the solo part would stand out from an eight-part tuba/euphonium ensemble. The second aspect was made easier by the fact that I was writing for Roger Bobo, a player with unparalleled technical virtuosity and power of tone, particularly in the high register. I knew it would be possible for me to write the solo tuba part above the euphoniums at times and get a successful balance.

The mood of the work is achieved by using some basic compositional devices. Repetitive ostinato figures and ascending lines represent, rather obviously perhaps, the eternal toil of Sisyphus. The solo part, virtuosic throughout, is rhythmically very complex against the simplicity of the accompanying parts. This represents the unrelenting torment in the mind of Sisyphus. The slow, tedious opening section shifts into a very fast section (the forces that will liberate Sisyphus in action!). This section becomes more and more frantic until, at last, in the final *maestoso*, dissonances resolve, rhythms simplify, the harmonic structure becomes more traditional, and Sisyphus is at last able to sing a song of exultation. It culminates in a high C (one octave above middle C) in the solo part that concludes the work.

Soliloquy—Peace in Our Time

Madison, WI: John D. Stevens, 1990.
Movements: One continuous movement
Instrumentation: Solo Instrument with Taped Acoustic Piano

Soliloquy is totally improvisational. There is no written music for the solo part, and the music on the tape was improvised as well. The piece was conceived and the tape was realized in the spring of 1990. I premiered it on a recital at the University of Wisconsin-Madison in April 1990. The inspiration for the work was the chain of incredible events in Europe and around the world in 1989 and 1990. Although I had the tuba in mind as the solo instrument, virtually any instrument could perform with the tape, since acoustic piano is the only taped sound used.

The tape lasts approximately nine minutes. Although it has periods of silence to allow the soloist to be heard alone, the taped music was realized in one continuous take. I simply sat at a piano in a recording studio, let my thoughts take over, and played. A soloist could approach performing the piece in the same way. Depending on how much improvising experience one had, a number of listenings and/or run-throughs would enhance a final performance. Each performance of this work will be different and unique.

Suite No. 1

N.p.: Cleveland Chamber Music Publishers, 1974.
Movements: I. Slow and rubato-fast
               II. Ponderous
               III. Slow and freely
               IV. March
               V. Slow and sombre-freely
Instrumentation: Tuba alone

Suite No. 1 was composed in 1974 while I was a graduate student at Yale and was my first original composition for tuba. I premiered the work myself and eventually recorded it on *Power*, an album of my own compositions (Mark Records No. 20699).

The piece was originally conceived as a musical representation of a day in the life of a child. The first movement evolves from a slow, muted (optional) awakening section into a very fast, rhythmically energetic section. The second movement, though marked "Ponderous," is still somewhat playful or whimsical. As is typical of all my music, the energy of the rhythmic activity is of prime importance.

The third movement is a restful, songlike one; however, a certain level of agitation is retained because the melody jumps all around, never going where the listener anticipates. This effect was achieved by writing a simple, traditional melody, then displacing every second or third note by an octave up or down.

The fourth movement is a march that continues the feel of the third movement by using widely spaced intervals throughout the thematic material.

The final movement is like a dream sequence. It recalls snippets of all the previous movements, but in a wilder and more agitated manner. It finally ends in a slow, muted passage, returning the listener to the opening material of the first movement, thus completing the cycle of "a day in the life."

After composing the work in such a programmatic fashion, I subsequently decided that the structure of the piece worked on its own, so I changed the title and eliminated any reference to the program in the published version.

Richard Stroud (b. 1929)

Richard Stroud is Chairman of the Music Department and a teacher of Concert Band and Jazz Studies in the Eureka (California) city schools.

Night Train for Tubas

Unpublished.
Movements: One movement
Instrumentation: Tuba, Euphonium, Bass, Piano, Guitar, and Drums

I have been involved in jazz studies for most of my teaching career. I have written for various jazz ensembles for 40 years, and when the tuba-jazz movement started in the late 1970s, it was like a breath of fresh air. Tuba ensembles were included in my jazz writing immediately.

Night Train for Tubas, written in 1980, is an arrangement for tuba ensemble on the old jazz standard. It includes a jazz rhythm section and emphasizes the blues idiom. It contains a completely open section for free improvisation, allowing any member of the tuba ensemble to really "spread out" for as long as practical. The tempo is a medium to a medium-slow groove, designed to uplift the whole ensemble. This arrangement can be played by two tubas and two euphoniums up to a balanced group of at least twenty.

It is designed to be a crowd pleaser and provide easy listening. It could be a very effective encore number as a change of pace on any serious program, or as a piece of music history on a complete jazz program.

A Variation of East African Calls

Eureka, CA: Richard Stroud, 1981.
Movements: One movement
Instrumentation: Tuba alone

This composition was written especially for R. Winston Morris at Tennessee Tech University, at Cookeville, in appreciation for the faith he had shown in other compositions by this writer. It is a virtuoso piece patterned on actual bird songs from East Africa, and it requires more than just the average ability and agility for the tuba. It is unaccompanied and designed to attract the above-average player. With multirhythms, it explores a number of the technical possibilities that exist on the tuba and definitely places it outside of the "oom-pah-pah" tradition. It is a short piece with allowance for a certain amount of freedom at the end, and it should provide an interesting, exciting addition to any tuba recital. If a number is needed to supply difficulty level, it is definitely a grade VI.

Donald Swann (b. 1923)

Donald Swann is an English pianist and co-composer, with the late Michael Flanders, of the long-running Broadway musical *At the Drop of a Hat.*

Two Moods for Tuba

New York: Chamber Music Library, 1961.
Movements: I. Elegy
                         II. Scherzo
Instrumentation: Tuba and Piano

Gerard Hoffnung thought the tuba the most marvelous thing in the world. He drew it continually for five years, then learned to play it. He played the Vaughan Williams *Tuba Concerto* at the Royal Festival Hall, and after that he was going over to conducting, but he tragically died. He told me that when he was asked to make brief appearances with his tuba he had a devil of a time deciding what to play, especially if the interview (radio, TV, or what have you) was before a non-long-haired audience. He besought me to write a "lighter" piece. This is it. Though Hoffnung never played it, Harvey Phillips did it brilliantly at sight in New York, and thus started it on its career.

   The "Elegy" is inspired by (but I hope not lifted from) the last bars of Honneger's *Third Symphony.* I love to see the tuba mute coming out, that socking great cork. The "Scherzo" is a skit, somewhat of a battle between the pianist and the tuba player for the right key. They both win.

Fred Tackett (b. 1945)

Fred Onstead Tackett, of Los Angeles, CA, is a member of the musical group Little Feat. He is a "Doctor of Rock'n'Roll, a Ph.D. in Swing, and a Master of Rhythm."

The Yellow Bird

Los Angeles: Hoceanna Music, 1972.
Movements: I. Fast
             II. Not so Fast
            III. Real Fast
Instrumentation: Solo Tuba, Bass, Drums, Electric Guitar, Electric Keyboard

The Yellow Bird was written for Roger Bobo in 1972. When I met Roger, I was working with the songwriter Jimmy Webb. The guys in the band and Roger became great friends, and we spent many many pleasant hours socializing at Jimmy's. Roger expressed an interest in playing with the band, but since he did not have a great deal of previous experience with jazz improvisation, we needed a written-out, structured piece of music with improvisational sections included for the rock'-n'rollers. I wrote *The Yellow Bird* to meet that need. The piece has been played many times over the years, and because of its improvisational nature, it is always different. The tuba part is pretty much written-out, except for a solo in the slow second movement, where I thought Roger should go for it! Everybody else's part is a combination of improvisation and written-out notes. However, I change my part all the time. I believe all the other rhythm section players tend to do the same thing after they become overly familiar (read, bored) with their part. I think this is a real good idea!

The first movement starts out with a rhythmic pulse from the bass and drums. The electric keyboard plays sustained clusters over this pulse. The tuba has a very rhythmic, eighth-note statement which lasts the first 40 measures. The guitar plays an introduction in F minor. The tuba now plays a very pretty melody over the minor groove. At letter C (bar 62), the guitar introduces a waltz with occasional bars of 4/4 alternating with the 3/4 bars. At bar 94 the tuba joins the guitar in harmony. At letter E everyone plays a rhythmic declaration, which is followed by two bars of drums. They then repeat the rhythm in another key. At letter F, the first theme is repeated, just to prove we are good boys and take this sonata stuff real serious.

There is a direct *segue* into the second movement, accomplished by a guitar solo with keyboard accompaniment. The piano then plays a vamp in 7/4, which introduces the groove for the second movement. The tuba really has a beautiful melody, if I do say so myself and I do. The melody ascends one note higher on each phrase for the first half of the melody and then descends in kind. At bar 35 the rhythm section plays a funky lick in unison and the melody repeats. At letter B, the first improvisational section occurs. Everyone plays a solo on the chord changes of the first 36 bars. After the solos, the melody is repeated, and second movement ends.

The third movement begins with the drum, guitar, and tuba. At bar 17, the tuba and drums play together in unison. This is followed by a furious rhythm from the bass, guitar, keyboards, and drums. The accompaniment and the melodic material are derived from a row rather than from traditional jazz chords. At letter D, a series of ninth chords is used for improvisation from the guitar, bass, and keyboards. The tuba solo is written-out. Following the second tuba solo, there is a *rubato* section featuring the tuba. On the record, this section ends with four tubas, overdubbed by Roger, playing an extended cadence, but this is not usually played by four tubas in a live situation.

Ralph Vaughan Williams
(1872–1958)

Concerto for Bass Tuba and Orchestra

London: Boosey & Hawkes, 1959.
Movements: I. Prelude—Allegro moderato
                      II. Romanza—Andante sostenuto
                      III. Rondo alla tedesca—Allegro
Instrumentation: Tuba and Orchestra

Besides notable concertos for violin and for piano, Ralph Vaughan Williams has enriched the literature of the concerto for lesser-known instruments—the harmonica and the bass tuba—raising them, too, to concerto rank.

The administrators of the London Symphony Orchestra felt that the Jubilee Celebrations of the Orchestra called for a work from one of England's foremost composers. A request was made of Ralph Vaughan Williams for a composition to honor the occasion. The composer responded with the *Tuba Concerto*, which is dedicated to the London Symphony Orchestra. In an analytical note he stated:

> The form of this concerto is nearer to the Bach form than that of the Viennese School (Mozart and Beethoven) though the first and last movements each finish up with an elaborate cadenza which allies the concerto to the Mozart-Beethoven form. The music is fairly simple and obvious and can probably be listened to without much previous explanation. The orchestration is that of the so-called Theatre Orchestra consisting of woodwinds, two each of horns, trumpets and trombones, timpani, percussion and strings.

The *Tuba Concerto* received its premiere in June 1954 at one of the London Symphony Orchestra's Jubilee Concerts. The soloist was Philip Catelinet—then tubist with the LSO, and the conductor was Sir John Barbirolli.

The work has been revised since its first publication through the combined services of Roy Douglas, Vaughan Williams's personal pianist-cum-editor, Christopher Morris of Oxford University Press, and the writer. It is hoped that these three, along with many interested performers, conductors, and teachers, have brought about a more correct edition, which is now available from Oxford University Press.

In private and rehearsal sessions with Vaughan Williams, Philip Catelinet was privileged to question him and receive pointers as to the work's creation and its performance. It was evidently composed very quickly. At their first meeting, the composer was adamant that he did not desire any suggestions for alterations in the music itself, other than in such matters as phrasing and slurs. A warning was given regarding the last movement, "Rondo a la Tedesca" (waltz rhythm), which he wished to be treated as a rather stately German waltz; definitely not to be hurried.

Program note by Philip Catelinet, Associate Professor of Music, Emeritus, at Carnegie-Mellon University, Pittsburgh, PA. He is honorary editor of *The Conductor* and a former pianist, tubist, trombonist, and euphoniumist of the BBC Military Band, the BBC Concert Orchestra, the London Symphony Orchestra, and the Philharmonic Orchestra.

[The following material was written by Ernest Bradbury and is reprinted from the Henry Wood Promenade Concerts Series program of July 25, 1955.]

The more enlightened readers of this note will not have forgotten the joyous adventure of *Tubby the Tuba*, as recounted by the inimitable Danny Kaye. Signor Pizzicato, it will be recalled (to say nothing of the rest of the orchestra), was both troubled and annoyed when Tubby wished he had a tune for himself—instead of that perpetual oompah. But they were excited enough when they heard Tubby's tune, after he had learnt it from the Bull-frog. And why not? Dr. Vaughan Williams, like the Bull-frog—but with rather more experience in creating good tunes—has also shown some concern for those instruments that are not, so to say, destined to be for solo performers. He manifestly enjoys the challenge offered by new problems of instrumental ensemble, and shows a craftsman's delight in solving, as they arise, new problems of texture. This is the opposite of a long-faced attitude to music. Three years ago a Prom audience heard his *Romance for Harmonica* for the first time. The *Tuba Concerto* (the first to be written for this instrument) received its premiere in June last year at one of the concerts given in celebration of the London Symphony Orchestra's Jubilee. Tonight's soloist, Philip Catelinet, also played it on that occasion.

Whatever problems the composer had to solve, listeners will find no difficulty in enjoying these three short movements. The first of them is perhaps not without a touch of humour, as the solo instrument dances genially along, enhancing or providing the suggestion of an oompah rhythm. Is the tuba a romantic instrument? After the cadenza to the first movement we may not think so: short acquaintance with the *Concerto's* second movement may change our opinion. The key is D major, the mood is lyrical and mellow, and the soloist has a tune—the like of which Tubby and the Bull-frog never dreamed of. Perhaps there is something reminiscent of a performing bear in the Rondo as the tuba is put through its paces. There is the suggestion of a waltz, not so clod-hopping as might be imagined, and again the soloist has his brief cadenza before the final bars.

Anthony Vazzana (b. 1922)

Anthony Vazzana is Professor of Theory and Composition at the University of Southern California, Los Angeles.

Cambi

Manuscript, 1978.
Movements: I. Toccata
                 II. Canzona
              III. Giga
Instrumentation: Tuba and Percussion

The three movements of *Cambi* exploit the broad technical and expressive capabilities of the two protagonists.

"Toccata," in sectional form, begins with the tuba stating and developing an aggressive fanfare motive, challenged by interjections from various percussion instruments, such as suspended cymbal, tuned drums, various idiophones, vibraphone, and marimba. This free, declamatory dialogue develops by using extended techniques, such as singing normally through the tuba, falsetto vocalizing, and microtonalism. Near the close of the "Toccata" there is a brief reference to the opening, which evolves into more frenetic gestures employing timbral trills and rapid scale passages. It ends with a sharp, staccato attack (*ff*) by both performers.

The through-composed "Canzona" begins slowly with a reflective theme in the low register of the tuba. It gradually increases in dynamic and emotional intensity as it ascends to the top register. Wind chimes provide a subtle and discreet rustling background. The movement ends with the tuba recalling the opening material in the lowest (pedal) register.

The highly rhythmical and energetic "Giga" is also through-composed and emphasizes both the virtuosity and the equality of the two partners. After an introductory suspended cymbal roll, the tuba launches into a rapid repeated-note figure shared with the vibraphone and later the marimba. Syncopation and rhythmic surprises build rapidly toward a frenzied *tremolando* climax in both parts, which is interrupted by a grand pause. Closing the movement is a soft double glissando executed in contrary motion by tuba and marimba.

Donald White (b. 1921)

Donald H. White is Chairman of the Department of Music and Professor of Composition at Central Washington University in Ellensburg.

Sonata for Tuba and Piano

Cleveland: Ludwig Music Publishing Co., 1979.
Movements: I. Adagio—Allegro
                II. Adagio affettuoso
                III. Presto giusto
Instrumentation: Tuba and Piano

The *Sonata for Tuba and Piano*, commissioned by Custom
Music Company in cooperation with the Tubists Universal
Brotherhood Association, was composed in 1978 and published the following year. Its premiere took place at the
University of Maryland on January 17, 1979, with several performances occurring soon afterward. Following completion of
its initial draft, the composer had the privilege of reviewing
the *Sonata* with Daniel Perantoni, then tubist-in-residence at
the University of Illinois. After some minor editing, the work
was forwarded to Ludwig Music Publishing Company for
printing.

The *Sonata* presents three movements in typically contrasting fast—slow—fast tempi, with each movement involving
brief introductory materials. The first movement is a simple
sonata form with inversion of themes A and B during the recapitulation. Melodic elements rely heavily on the minor
second plus its major seventh inversion and octave expansions.
Rhythmically, the movement is quite straightforward with
occasional use of asymmetric eighth-note beaming. The development utilizes elements from both thematic ideas, with
antiphonal byplay between tuba and piano.

The second movement again involves intervals of the second
together with their inversions set against arpeggiated and block
chordal structures, which are both bi- and polychordal. The
movement is essentially an ABA formal design, and the Coda
recalls B and then A in truncated form.

The third movement is a simple rondo structure with two
thematic elements featuring an alteration between 7/8 and 2/4
meters. Theme A greatly resembles the first theme in Move-

ment I, while theme B is drawn directly from the introduction
to the first movement. Taken together, the thematic elements
of the third movement create a cyclic effect in the sonata's
formal design. Harmonic elements are quartal bi-chords stated
in blocks or with rhythmic motivation. The *Sonata for Tuba
and Piano* was conceived as a work for two instruments of
equal importance.

Alec Wilder (1907–1980)

Sonata for Tuba and Piano

New York: Mentor Music, Inc., 1968.
Movements: I. Quarter note = 92
               II. Allegro—Swing
               III. Andante
               IV. Allegro
Instrumentation: Tuba and Piano

The *Sonata for Tuba and Piano* was composed by Alec Wilder
in 1964 at the request of Harvey Phillips. Since it was one of
the first extended works for this instrumental combination,
Wilder was able to explore freely new relationships between
the soaring melodies, as well as provide sonorous bass lines in
support of the piano's harmonies.

The first movement begins with a simple, plaintive statement by the piano, which later serves as the accompaniment
for the entrance of the tuba. This opening motive recurs
periodically throughout the first movement and makes a fleeting appearance in the third movement, but, interestingly, it is
never taken up by the tuba.

The second movement is a scherzo with two alternating
sections and a contrasting interlude. The first section consists
of a wide-ranging tuba motive, accompanied by a jazzy piano
ostinato. The second section, in a slow blues tempo, has the
flavor of "stripper music." The interlude between Tempo I

and Swing Tempo recalls material from the first movement and gives a foretaste of the third movement.

The third movement is the spiritual core of the work. The tuba spins out long, expressive lines against poignant harmonies. There are clear motivic and emotional links to the first movement.

The fourth movement is built on a jagged motive in changing meters, first stated by the piano. The atmosphere is brusque and severe, and the movement ends with a characteristic "door slam."

Suite No. 1 for Tuba and Piano (Effie Suite)

Newtown Center, MA: Margun Music, Inc., 1968.
Movements: I. Effie Chases a Monkey
              II. Effie Falls in Love
             III. Effie Goes Folk Dancing
              IV. Effie Takes a Dancing Lesson
               V. Effie Joins the Carnival
              VI. Effie Sings a Lullaby
Instrumentation: Tuba and Piano

This popular suite was written at the request of Clark Galehouse of Crest Records, for a children's album. It was originally scored for tuba, piano, drums, bass, and percussion, including xylophone. It was later arranged for tuba and piano, and it is this version which is most frequently performed. The piece is a suite depicting six episodes in a day in the life of a charming elephant named Effie. It was originally written for Harvey Phillips, who has said the following in the liner notes to Golden Crest RE 7054:

> I believe Mr. Wilder was successful in musically documenting these imaginary events without the usual insult to the instrument occasioned by almost every other application of the tuba as a hippopotamus, whale, elephant or other large creature. Rather than play on making the instrument and its characterization one of clumsiness and retardation, he maintained dignity, charm and warmth.

The titles of each movement are self-explanatory; however, it may be of interest to note a few of the humorous touches. At the end of the first movement, "Effie Chases a Monkey," it appears that Effie, hot in pursuit, miscalculates and runs into a tree. In "Effie Takes a Dancing Lesson," the piano assumes the role of dance instructor. During the lesson, Effie loses the downbeat and misplaces a few notes, for which she is severely reprimanded. And of course, at the close of such a busy day of activity, it is not surprising that Effie sings herself to sleep.

Suite for French Horn, Tuba and Piano

New York: Wilder Music, 1971.
Movements: I. Energetic (Maestoso)
              II. Elegy (Pesante)
             III. Relaxed (In a jazz manner)
              IV. Berceuse (Andante) [for Carol]
               V. Finale (Alla caccia)
Instrumentation: French Horn, Tuba, and Piano

The impetus for the composition of this work, one of the first ever written for this instrumental combination, came from Clark Galehouse, then president of Crest Records. Having recorded both tubist Harvey Phillips and hornist John Barrows, he was struck by the similarities in sound and phrasing between the two artists. He mentioned this to Alec Wilder, and a project was created to bring these two artists together. The resulting *Suite* was first performed during the summer of 1963, while both musicians were teaching at the University of Wisconsin.[1]

Of his compositional process, Alec Wilder explained:

> I work almost wholly intuitively. I have a few little technical things I use, but I believe that technique is the composer's secret. . . . I have an innate sense of order, balance, and shape. I know most of the rules of counterpoint, although I never studied theory. When I start a piece, I try and find a melodic idea that I consider seminal, that I think will hold up. Then I find secondary themes as I move along. I work at the piano

more often than not. I will play the parts I've written very slowly, and I'll work as hard on eight sixteenth notes, trying to get that right balance and flow and feeling, as I will on an entire piece.[2]

Wilder's motivic approach to composition can be seen clearly in the five-movement *Suite for French Horn, Tuba and Piano*. The first movement begins with a vigorous motive, presented individually by the tuba, horn, and piano. This motive is developed, and a countermotive is introduced. The second theme, presented by the horn, is more lyrical, providing a contrast to the first section.

The second movement, "Elegy," begins with a statement by the piano, in bare octaves, of the countermotive from the first movement. The atmosphere is desolate and dark. Whitney Balleitt observed that in this movement "the two horns move in subtle, close counterpoint in such a way that it is sometimes difficult to tell one from the other, Wilder having written high for the tuba and low for the horn."[3] The movement builds to a tremendous climax, both horns climbing to the extremes of their registers.

The third movement is built on a jazz motive, punctuated by rests, first stated by the tuba. The rests are filled by offbeat rhythmic interjections from the piano. Later the roles are reversed, and the horn is included in the exchange. This jazzy material alternates with lyrical interludes in a slower, sustained tempo.

The fourth movement, a lullaby, opens with a gentle duet for the two horns. The motive is developed, then a quiet rocking rhythm is established by the piano. After a fleeting reference by the horn to the opening motive of the first movement, a strikingly beautiful idea is presented, first by the piano, then by the two horns.

The final movement, a sort of galop, makes extensive use of imitative counterpoint. The first motive is presented in fugal style. A second motive, consisting of wide intervals and repeated notes, is stated first aggressively, then tenderly. The tuba alone presents a slower version of the opening motive, leading to the recapitulation, and ultimately, to a characteristic "door-slamming" finale.

NOTES

1. James T. Maher, liner notes, Golden Crest RE 7018.
2. Whitney Balliett, *Alec Wilder and His friends* (New York: Da Capo Press, 1983), p. 201.
3. Ibid, p. 186.

Program notes by Steven Harlos, Coordinator of Accompanying at the College of Music, University of North Texas, Denton.

Rolf Wilhelm (b. 1927)

Rolf Wilhelm is a conductor and composer living in Grünwald, Germany.

Concertino for Tuba and Winds

In manuscript.
Movements: I. Moderato deciso
          II. Andante lirico
          III. Allegro comodo
Instrumentation: Tuba and Wind Ensemble; also available for Tuba and Piano

The *Concertino for Tuba and Winds* was composed in 1983 at the request of my friend Robert Tucci. The first performance took place on June 23, 1983, during the International Tuba and Euphonium Conference at the University of Maryland. Mr. Tucci was the soloist, accompanied by the United States Air Force Band of Washington, D.C., under the direction of Col. Arnald Gabriel.

My intention was to create an easily comprehended, uncomplicated work of a pleasant nature for the tuba, that fascinating instrument with an enormous range of more than four octaves. Further, I wished to contradict in a jovial manner the ever-prevailing prejudice that the tuba was an uncultivated monster suitable only for march music. The second movement in particular proves how expressive and lyrical this transsubstantial instrument can be.

Movement I, "Moderato deciso": This Classical sonata movement utilizes an accented, rhythmic main theme, which alternates with another of melodic nature. Short reminiscences of ragtime rhythms and considerable configuration show the agility of the instrument. The cadenza flows into a 6/8 coda, which ends in a short dialogue between piccolo and tuba.

Movement II, "Andante lirico": Music in 3/4 time contains beautiful, lyric melodies featuring various instruments of the woodwind section as well as the solo tuba.

Movement III, "Allegro commodo": This light-hearted movement is sometimes playful, sometimes bombastic. Various soloistic passages within the orchestra are interwoven with the solo tuba's melodies and the cadenza, all of which are derived from a portly and comfortable 6/8 theme typical of the instrument. Suggestions of Bavarian folk music alternate with lyrical passages and virtuosic episodes. The cadenza, a dialogue with other instruments, demonstrates again the full range of four octaves. The main theme is presented one last time with harmonic variation, and the work ends in a furious stretto, *fortissimo*.

Translated by Robert Tucci, Principal Tubist, Bavarian State Opera Orchestra, Munich, Germany.

John Williams (b. 1932)

John Williams is the Music Director of the Boston Pops and composer of many movie soundtracks, including *Star Wars*, *Return of the Jedi*, *The Empire Strikes Back*, *Close Encounters of the Third Kind*, and *Indiana Jones*.

Tuba Concerto

Secaucus, NJ: Warner Brothers Music, 1985.
Movements: I. Allegro moderato
                II. Andante
                III. Allegro molto
Instrumentation: Tuba and Orchestra

In addition to the film music for which he is so widely known,
John Williams has written many concert pieces, including two
symphonies and concertos for violin and flute. For the 350th
anniversary of the city of Boston, he composed the *Jubilee 350
Fanfare*; and for the Boston Pops he wrote *Esplanade Overture*
and *Pops on the March*. Additional concert works include *Essay
for Strings* and numerous chamber pieces. The *Tuba Concerto*,
written in 1984–85 to celebrate the 100th anniversary of the
Boston Pops, was premiered on May 8, 1985 by that orchestra
with Chester Schmitz, principal tubist of the Boston Symphony
Orchestra and the Boston Pops. The following information
about the work appeared in the program booklet for that performance:

> The *Concerto* is laid out in the normal three movements, but
> with no pause between the movements. The opening "Allegro
> moderato" introduces the soloist at once against a gently rock-
> ing pulse in the strings, harp and upper woodwinds. The tuba's
> tune is taken up by the other instruments before the tuba intro-
> duces a second theme, also in the rocking 12/8 of the opening;
> this sets off a more elaborate solo passage culminating in an un-
> usual cadenza for the tuba companionably accompanied by all
> four horns. The opening rocking figure returns for a single brief
> statement.
>   An English horn solo introduces the "Andante," [which
> grows] in lines that are increasingly ornate and finally pass to
> the solo flute. This, too, climbs expressively in an elegant arc.
> When the tuba enters with its own decorated line, it engages in
> a brief dialogue with the flute. A new rhythmic section begins
> (*Poco più mosso*), with the tuba syncopated against a steady beat

in the orchestra. A return of the opening ideas with tuba, English horn and flute die away in a sustained high string chord.

The finale begins at once (Allegro molto); here the entire brass section sets up the rhythmic pulse that runs throughout the movement, sometimes in sections for full orchestra, sometimes in quieter dialogue, as between tuba and harp with pizzicato punctuation from strings. The woodwinds and the trumpet choir assert themselves. Then after a full orchestral interjection and one last bit of harp/tuba dialogue, the full orchestra brings in a rousing close.

© Boston Symphony Orchestra. Reprinted by permission.

Marilyn J. Ziffrin (b. 1926)

Marilyn J. Ziffrin is Professor Emeritus at New England College, Henniker, NH.

Four Pieces for Tuba

San Diego, CA: Music Graphics Press, 1982.
Movements: I. Andante
                II. Allegro
              III. Largo
              IV. Vivace
Instrumentation: Tuba alone

These pieces were commissioned by Barton Cummings. When Mr. Cummings wrote to me explaining the myriad possibilities of his instrument, it seemed only natural to me to write a set of pieces that would show off the capabilities of the instrument while keeping in mind that the pieces would also have musical value of their own.

The four pieces follow the age-old pattern of slow—fast—slow—fast, and generally each develops out of its opening motive. There is no extramusical meaning in any of them. The first movement is like an opening proclamation; the fast second movement is a show piece for the performer; the third, a *largo*, is more introspective and personal; while the final fast and rhythmical piece is more lighthearted and dancelike and contains some shifting meter patterns.

PART TWO

Composer Profiles

Paul Hindemith's Place in Twentieth-Century Music (1895–1963)

David Neumeyer, Professor of Music, Indiana University, Bloomington

After World War I, Richard Strauss still regarded himself as the grand old man among contemporary German composers. In the summer of 1921 he visited the first of a series of annual contemporary music festivals held in Donaueschingen, a small southwestern city blessed with an arts-loving (and generous) prince. Strauss made the mistake of criticizing the rather brash young Paul Hindemith, whose *Second String Quartet* had just been given an enthusiastic reception. "Why do you compose atonal music?" asked Strauss. "You have plenty of talent." The young man's reply was simply, "You make your music, and I'll make mine."

In the 1920s Hindemith's compositional style was often described as atonal (and not just by his critics). Even twenty years later, a *Time* magazine writer felt free to describe him as "Germany's leading atonal composer, who was driven from his homeland by the Nazis"; and later still, the 1958 premiere of a symphony commissioned by the Pittsburgh Orchestra inspired a cartoonist to depict two symphony patrons, one examining her program with a sour stare while the other said: "Now, Claire, just because it's Hindemith doesn't mean there's payola involved."

In fact, during the 1920s it was common to regard "atonal" as synonymous with "modern" or "avant-garde," which usually referred rather vaguely to anything outside of settled, later

An earlier version of these remarks appeared as "Paul Hindemith: Musician's Musician" in the program magazine of the San Francisco Symphony Orchestra, November 1987.

nineteenth-century style norms. In this sense only, "atonal" might be an appropriate tag for Hindemith's early music. During the 1950s the term came to connote specifically traits of pre–World War I musical expressionism: a narrowly defined style characterized by very chromatic, often rather tortured and angular melodic lines; dissonant, added-note harmonies; dynamic extremes; and short-breathed phrases. Hindemith did write some music of this kind, mainly for intense slow movements, such as those in the *Kammermusik* series (1921–27) or the *Viola Sonata*, Op. 25, No. 4 (1922), and for the two Passion songs in the song cycle *Das Marienleben* (1922–23), but his compositional manner was essentially eclectic. His earliest compositions (before 1920), mainly instrumental sonatas and songs, show rather little influence from Schoenberg, and quite a bit from Brahms, Reger, Schreker, and Debussy. After 1920, one can readily hear traces of Stravinsky and Bartók as well (for example, in *Kammermusik, No. 1* and the *Suite*, Op. 26). What surprises one in listening to this music, however, is the strength of the compositional personality that shows through it and the early age at which Hindemith found his own voice— by early 1923, his style is consistent and unmistakable.

Strauss obviously thought the late-Romantic style of Hindemith's conservatory training was good enough and that the younger composer should stick to it, but Hindemith quite as obviously intended to do nothing of the kind. Just turning 24 when World War I ended, he was caught up in the anti-Romantic sentiment and vigorous experimentation that followed. The string quartet played in Donaueschingen was his first real success as a composer, and it quickly won him a reputation which a prodigious series of works as quickly enhanced. He was well known for his ability to compose music rapidly and under adverse conditions—such as during train trips. Four of five movements of a solo cello sonata, for example, were composed in one day at Donaueschingen. (The last one was written shortly thereafter on the train back to Frankfurt.) Another feat of this sort finally allowed Strauss to get his own back: At a 1924 summer festival, he asked Hindemith how long it had taken him to compose the piece he had just heard. "Four days," said Hindemith, to which Strauss replied, "That's what I thought."[1]

It undoubtedly helped the advancement of Hindemith's career that the *ad hoc* group assembled to premiere the quartet at Donaueschingen began touring as a professional ensemble a year later, under the name Amar Quartet (after its first violinist, Licco Amar). Until it was disbanded in 1929, this quartet was a strong and very active proponent of contemporary string music of all styles. Among their accomplishments was the first recording of Bartók's *Second String Quartet* in 1925, a work they had performed fifteen times in concert. According to Hindemith's personal records, they performed Schoenberg's *First String Quartet* more than 30 times, as well as chamber works by Reger, Debussy, Korngold, Honegger, Hába, Malipiero, Webern, and many others.[2]

Throughout Hindemith's life, composition and performance were always tightly linked. A brilliant violinist with wide performance experience, Hindemith was appointed concertmaster of the Frankfurt State Opera orchestra at the age of nineteen (1915). Some indication of his skill can be seen from his own account of his audition. The conductor, Willem Mengelberg, had already chosen his own candidate and only grudgingly heard the young Hindemith, who was given an extremely difficult passage from a Strauss opera to sight-read. He negotiated the passage without apparent difficulty, and Mengelberg was forced to give him the job. After the Amar Quartet disbanded, Hindemith formed a trio with Berlin colleagues Szymon Goldberg and Emmanuel Feuermann and also toured as a concert violist. Later, he turned to orchestral conducting. Add to all this his formation of a *collegium musicum* and his participation in its concerts at Yale in the 1940s and one can see that Hindemith was never far from active music making.

The matter-of-factness that was a true hallmark of his personal and musical style thus partly obscured the truth about Hindemith: that music ran so strongly through and throughout him that it reached from the reflexes of everyday life to his deepest philosophical and religious impulses. Like Stravinsky's show of cold-fish objectivity in his book *Poetics of Music*, Hindemith's matter-of-factness has an element of public face, of personal advertising, about it. Hindemith was quite capable of both expressive warmth and spiritual depth, as his music clearly shows, but he loathed any tendency to wallow.

Partly as a result of this objectivity, partly because of his love for both clear forms and contrapuntal display, Hindemith has often been described as a neoclassical composer, but the several connotations of that old term do not really apply to him very well—neither the reactionary nationalism of Italian composer Alfredo Casella, nor Busoni's *junge Klassizität*, nor the Stravinsky side in the Schoenberg-Stravinsky partisan polemic of the 1920s and 30s. Stravinsky, with his roots in a Franco-Russian tradition and specifically in ballet, suffered from "musical kleptomania," as he himself called it, which led him to appropriate earlier styles, mannerisms, even actual pieces (as in *Pulcinella*), and to reinterpret them by distortion with the musical equivalent of Cubist multiple perspective. Schoenberg, on the other hand, with his twelve-tone technique sought to institutionalize the prewar expressionism which remained the basis of his style, and he opposed serious German philosophical idealism to French frivolity when he complained that the neoclassicists were merely fiddling with style while they ignored essential ideas.

For Hindemith, the object all along was synthesis: of diatonic and chromatic materials, tonal and atonal methods, French and German styles, twenties' cleverness with the gravity of a sense of Western music's traditions. His orientation toward both a contemporary musical aesthetic and the preservation of a tradition was fundamentally positive. Throughout his career Hindemith searched for a way out of the Romantic-Modernist dialectic. To the extent he succeeded (and he didn't entirely), he did so by means of the most thorough-going historicism of any composer in this century, the one musician to whom historian Peter Burger's term "historical avant-garde" really applies. This is not to say that Hindemith merely imitated historical styles and techniques. Instead, he synthesized them with all the wit, optimism, sympathy, and seriousness of a distinct and confident compositional personality. In the end, he came to see the need for this dialogue with history in ethical terms.

The rest of his career may be said to follow directly from that first burst of creative activity in the early 1920s, but he was at the height of his powers in the decade 1935–45. To a considerable extent, this is due to the richly creative aftermath of his opera *Mathis der Maler* (1932–34), the work he frankly regarded as his masterpiece. Among the products of these years are a surprisingly large number of orchestral compositions: the revised version of *Das Marienleben*, the piano cycle *Ludus Tonalis*, and the majority of his sonatas for solo instruments and piano. This last group is a varied lot— some are virtuoso works (especially the string sonatas), some are *Spielmusik* that nevertheless can have their serious, even autobiographical sides (as in the *Trumpet Sonata*), and one even originated as a class exercise at Yale (the *English Horn Sonata*). Having been forced finally to emigrate from Germany in 1938, Hindemith settled down in Switzerland to compose (among other works) two wind sonatas. He wrote three further sonatas in the fall of 1939. As a result, Schott publisher Willy Strecker suggested mischievously that he was "willing, as a spur to your imagination, to send you a list of instruments which have perhaps escaped your eagle eye."[3] In response, Hindemith revealed his reasons for all this activity:

> You might wonder why I seem to be writing sonatas for every one of the wind instruments. I have long had the idea of writing a series of these pieces. In the first place, except for a few classical compositions, there is nothing really practical available for these instruments, and although it may not be of immediate market value to expand this repertoire, in the long term it should be profitable. Secondly, I am enjoying this work tremendously, because I am very interested in wind instruments. Lastly, the pieces serve as technical exercises for the great coup I hope to bring off next spring: [the opera] *Die Harmonie der Welt*.[4]

Hindemith seems to have more or less abandoned the sonata series after 1943, but he did compose three further works—for cello, for double bass, and for tuba, in 1948, 1949, and 1955 respectively. Had a Yale colleague not demurred, there might also have been a bass clarinet sonata.[5]

After World War II, things did not go as well as one might have expected. To be sure, Hindemith was well settled in his

academic position at Yale, he held his compositional reputation, by then worldwide, and he kept as busy as ever. But by
about 1950, he seemed a bit out of tune with the times. He
had refused to return to his homeland after the war to be the
"grand old man" among modern German composers, thus
forfeiting any leadership role and in fact causing some re-
sentment. (Instead, he moved back to Switzerland in 1953 and
took up a second career as a conductor.) His catalogue of
works, like that of Darius Milhaud, a French contemporary
aesthetically close to Hindemith, suddenly seemed too large
for a modern composer, whose alienation was to be expressed
in a tortured handful of highly polished pieces. The model for
composition became the martyred Anton Webern, and it did
not take long before Hindemith came to suffer by comparison:
his work was too accessible, too moderate in technique and
expression, too routine, etc. And, of course, for nearly 30 years
Hindemith had denounced the serial techniques that were in
high vogue after about 1955. (Actually, he did briefly experi-
ment with those techniques in private, and the results do have
some effect on the first movement of the *Tuba Sonata* and on
the finale of the *Pittsburgh Symphony* (1958.[6])

The post-Webern manner turned rather quickly from its
namesake's exceedingly refined, abstract mysticism into
mandarin formalism, and eventually it became a mainly
academic closed shop. In this kind of environment, Hindemith's aesthetic of accessibility and love of music making had
little place. But time and further changes of fashion have
rendered that generation's rhetoric obsolete, too, so that we can
hear the work of a wider range of twentieth-century composers
with more reflection and not such quick judgment. If Hindemith's music is sometimes understated in its manner and
method (not so emotionally demonstrative as it might be, not
showing off his superb orchestration skill as much as it might,
not drawing out forms to the limits of their possibilities), it is
on the other hand a music which always has meaning, both in-
tellectual and emotional, and always brings that meaning forth
clearly and cleanly.

NOTES

1. The Strauss anecdotes recounted here were taken from Geoffrey Skelton, *Paul Hindemith: The Man behind the Music* (New York: Crescendo, 1975), pp. 71–72, 75.

2. See the facsimile in Andres Briner, Dieter Rexroth, and Giselher Schubert, *Paul Hindemith: Leben und Werk in Bild und Text* (Zurich: Atlantis/Mainz: Schott, 1988), pp. 111ff. For more on the relationship between Hindemith and Schoenberg, see David Neumeyer and Giselher Schubert, "Schoenberg and Hindemith," *Journal of the Arnold Schoenberg Institute* 13/1 (1990):3–46.

3. Willy Strecker to Hindemith, [November?] 1939, cited in translation in Skelton, p. 164.

4. Hindemith to Willy Strecker, November 20, 1939, cited in Jolena Geldenhuys, "The Late Sonata Works by Paul Hindemith (1895–1963): Chronological Perspective on the 26 Sonatas Written between 1935 and 1955," *Ars Nova* (University of South Africa) 20 (1988):16–17 (translation edited by the present author; the final clause is taken from the translation by Geoffrey Skelton in *Paul Hindemith*, p. 164).

5. Luther Noss, *Paul Hindemith in the United States* (Urbana: University of Illinois Press, 1989), pp. 131–32.

6. See David Neumeyer, *The Music of Paul Hindemith* (New Haven: Yale University, 1986), p. 242; and facsimiles of Hindemith's sketches for the *Tuba Sonata* in David Neumeyer, "Hindemiths Auseindersetzung mit der Reihentechnik," *Musiktheorie* 2/1 (1987): 58ff.

Vincent Persichetti
(1915–1987)

The Staff of Theodore Presser Company, Bryn Mawr, PA, Arnold Broido, President

There have been few more universally admired twentieth-century American composers than Vincent Persichetti. His contributions have enriched the entire musical literature, and his influence as performer and teacher is immeasurable.

Born in Philadelphia in 1915, Persichetti began his musical life at the age of five, first studying piano, then organ, double bass, tuba, theory, and composition. By the age of eleven, he was paying for his own musical education and helping to support himself by performing professionally as an accompanist, radio staff pianist, orchestra member, and church organist. At sixteen, he was appointed organist and choir director for the Arch Street Presbyterian Church in Philadelphia, a post he held for nearly twenty years. A virtuoso pianist and organist, he combined extraordinary versatility with an osmotic musical mind, and his earliest published works, written when he was fourteen, exhibit mastery of form, medium, and style.

Concurrent with these early activities, Persichetti was a student in the Philadelphia public schools and received a thorough musical education at the Combs College of Music, where he earned a Mus. B. degree in 1935 under Russell King Miller, his principal composition teacher. From the age of twenty, Persichetti was simultaneously head of the theory and composition departments at Combs College, a conducting major with Fritz Reiner at the Curtis Institute, and a piano major with Olga Samaroff at the Philadelphia Conservatory, in addition to studying composition with a number of important American composers. He received a Diploma in Conducting from Curtis Institute and Mus. M. and Mus. D. degrees from the Philadelphia Conservatory.

In 1941 Persichetti was appointed head of the theory and composition departments at the Philadelphia Conservatory. In the same year he married pianist Dorothea Flanagan. A daughter, Lauren, was born in 1944, and a son, Garth, in 1946. In 1947 he joined the faculty of the Juilliard School of Music, assuming chairmanship of the Composition Department in 1963. Persichetti was appointed Editorial Director of the music publishing firm of Elkan-Vogel, Inc. in 1952.

Over the years, Vincent Persichetti was accorded many honors by the artistic and academic communities, including several honorary Doctor of Music degrees, honorary membership in numerous musical fraternities, and all manner of awards. He was the recipient of three Guggenheim Fellowships, two grants from the National Foundation on the Arts and Humanities, and one from the National Institute of Arts and Letters, of which he was a member. He received some 100 commissions from various orchestras, universities, and individual performers, and appeared as guest conductor, lecturer, and composer at over 200 universities. Wide coverage by TV and news media of the premiere of his *A Lincoln Address* helped to focus worldwide attention on his music.

Persichetti composed for nearly every musical medium. More than 120 of his works are published, and many of these are available on records. Though he never specifically composed "educational" music, many of his smaller pieces are suitable for teaching purposes. His piano music, a complete body of literature in itself, consists of six sonatinas, three volumes of poems, a concerto and a concertino for piano and orchestra, serenades, a four-hand concerto, a two-piano sonata, twelve solo piano sonatas, and various shorter works. His keyboard virtuosity led him to produce nine organ works, including the intriguing *Sonatina for Organ, Pedals Alone* and the dramatic *Shimah B'Koli* (Psalm 130), as well as nine sonatas for harpsichord.

Persichetti's style of orchestral writing reflected his considerable talent and experience as a conductor. His *Fourth, Fifth* (*Symphony for Strings*), and *Eighth Symphonies* have made their way into the repertoire of major American symphonic ensembles. The *Seventh Symphony* was a very personal statement and is a symphonic development of materials from his small choral book *Hymns and Responses for the Church Year*. Another large important orchestral work, commissioned for the Philadelphia Orchestra, is *Sinfonia: Janiculum*, written while Persichetti was in Rome on his second Guggenheim Fellowship. The most famous of his smaller orchestral works, and one firmly established in American symphonic literature, is *The Hollow Men*, for trumpet and string orchestra, a delicate evocation of the T. S. Eliot poem. Three of his last commissions were the *English Horn Concerto* (New York Philharmonic), *Flower Songs: Cantata No. 6* (Michael Korn and the Philadelphia Singers), and *Chorale Prelude: Give Peace, Oh God* (Ann Arbor chapter of the American Guild of Organists).

Persichetti's instrumental compositions include two unique series: one comprises fifteen different works, each entitled *Serenade* for such diverse media as piano duet, flute and harp, solo tuba, orchestra, band, two recorders, two clarinets, and a trio consisting of trombone, viola, and cello. The series of 25 pieces, each entitled *Parable*, occupied Persichetti for some time. He also wrote four string quartets, a piano quintet, solo sonatas for violin and cello, *Infanta Marina* for viola and piano, *Little Recorder Book*, and *Masques* for violin and piano, to name just a few.

Persichetti's unusual feeling for poetry produced numerous vocal and choral compositions of remarkably high literary and music quality. His greatest solo vocal work is undoubtedly *Harmonium*, an impressive cycle of twenty closely interrelated songs to poems by Wallace Stevens.

Though not of the same magnitude as *Harmonium*, Persichetti's other vocal compositions exhibit a unique wedding of text and music, which sets them apart from most other composers' efforts in this genre. His choral output ranges from small works—such as *Proverb*, for mixed voices; *Song of Peace*, for male chorus and piano; *Spring Cantata*, for women's voices and piano—through larger works: *Mass*, for mixed chorus a capella; *Winter Cantata*, for women's voices, flute, and marimba; and *Glad and Very*, for two-part mixed, women's, or men's voices and piano. His large-scale sacred and secular works include: *The Pleiades*, for chorus, trumpet, and string orchestra; *Celebrations*, for chorus and wind ensemble; and what Persichetti considered his magnum opus, *The Creation*, a huge work for vocal quartet, chorus, and orchestra with texts drawn from mythological, scientific, poetic, and biblical sources. The small but significant choral book *Hymns and Responses for the Church Year* has already been influential in breathing a new spirit into twentieth-century hymnody.

More than any other major American composer, Persichetti poured his talents into the literature for wind band. From the *Serenade for Ten Wind Instruments*, Op. 1, to the *Parable for Band*, Op. 121, he provided performers and audiences with a body of music of unparalleled excellence. Of his fourteen band works, four are of major proportions: *Masquerade, Parable, A Lincoln Address*, and *Symphony for Band*. Although of lesser compositional importance, the *Divertimento* is nevertheless one of the most widely performed works in the entire repertoire.

In addition to his exhaustive compositional efforts, Persichetti found time to write one of the definitive books on modern compositional techniques, *Twentieth-Century Harmony: Creative Aspects and Practice* (New York: W.W. Norton, 1961), and essays in two books by Robert Hines on twentieth-century choral music and twentieth-century orchestral music (Norman: University of Oklahoma Press, 1963 and 1970). He also co-authored a biography of William Schuman (New York: G. Schirmer, 1954).

To a new, adventurous generation of composer—fortunately, large and musically eloquent—Persichetti was a teacher *par excellence* and a highly lucid theorist. In both capacities his great artistry was ever clear and impressive, providing an example of dynamic leadership for those who encountered his genius.

Remembering Halsey Stevens (1908–1989)

Morten Lauridsen, Professor and Chair of Theory and Composition, University of Southern California

I first met Halsey Stevens in his second-floor corner studio in Widney Hall on the USC campus in the Fall of 1963. Seated near his grand piano, piled high with his own published compositions, Stevens greeted me warmly and inquired about my journey south from Oregon, the piano repertoire I had recently performed, and my knowledge of contemporary scores.

Like many other aspiring composers, I had been drawn to Stevens by his reputation as an inspiring and effective teacher and by his respected international standing in musicology and composition. Over the next 25 years, I was privileged to become his friend and colleague and to assist him in the completion, orchestration, and editing of his final works. When Halsey Stevens succumbed in January 1989 to the effects of Parkinson's disease, shortly after celebrating his eightieth birthday, contemporary music lost one of its most eloquent and significant voices and Los Angeles a beloved and reassuring presence.

Stevens first attracted notice in the early 1940s, when Pierre Monteux invited him to conduct his *First Symphony* with the San Francisco Symphony, a work highly praised by the eminent critic Alfred Frankenstein. Joining the USC Faculty in 1946, Stevens soon established and became Chairman of the Department of Composition, holding that position until his retirement in 1976.

Halsey was an extremely prolific composer: more than 150 of his compositions, for virtually all media save opera and electronics, were published, and twenty were recorded. Intensely self-critical, he also withdrew dozens of his works during his career, marking each with a large "W" on the cover. Much of his music is characterized by a lean, Yankee sound—melodically and harmonically direct and open, imbued with a strong rhythmic vitality, architecturally clear, and cast overall within a carefully worked-out tonal framework. He had a distinct lyric gift and delighted in weaving complex contrapuntal lines that seemed to flow effortlessly. Above all he valued the final profile of a work, what he called the "sense of inevitability, of having to be written in the shape eventually attained." Long-time friend Wallace Berry writes of Stevens's "trait of creative integrity and depth of conviction . . . an unswerving accord with long established values affirmed by underlying intent in every note he has written."

Stevens firmly believed in creating music that was idiomatic and gracious for the performer and communicated with, rather than alienated, the listener. In his essay "A Composer Looks at Himself," he said, "I hope . . . that the music I write, fashionable or unfashionable, simple or complex, is capable of giving pleasure to some few people. Any future reward is an added bonus." Our rewards include his *Symphonic Dances* and *Sinfonia Breve*, the brilliant *Clarinet Concerto*, sonatas for all the principal orchestral instruments, the *Ballad of William Sycamore* and the *Magnificat*, over 100 songs, dozens of chamber works, and, of course, *Go, Lovely Rose*.

As his own catalogue grew, Stevens noticed similarities in aspects of his compositional approach and that of Bela Bartók. He began intensive research into Bartók's music, even learning Hungarian and retracing Bartók's sojourns through Europe, resulting in the 1953 publication of *The Life and Music of Béla Bartók*. In elegant prose he wrote:

> Had he not come quite by chance into contact with Magyar peasant music, Bartók would probably have continued in the neo-Hungarian tradition of Liszt and Erkel, the one molding his ideas in Germanic style, the other leaning toward the Italianate. But once having discovered the existence of a deep layer of native ore beneath the pyrites of Gypsy ornamentation, he set out in 1905 to mine it.

Stevens's book was the first major study of the composer and remains a standard work in musicology. He also contributed dozens of scholarly articles to music journals, lectured at over 60 universities, wrote program notes for the Los Angeles Philharmonic and Coleman Concert series, and was visiting composer at numerous institutions, including Yale. Two Guggenheim Fellowships and grants from the Fromm Foundation and the National Endowment of the Arts were among his many honors.

Stevens's graduate classes in composition and the music of Bartók were legendary for their depth and painstaking thoroughness and for his skill in patiently guiding his students through the mysteries and wonderment of the composition and analytical process.

Beyond Halsey's immense musical achievements, the man himself was held in an esteem bordering on reverence by his colleagues. He generated a quiet integrity and warmth and an endearing gentleness. He loved growing things and knew the Latin names for most of them. He collected exotic bells on his world travels, savoring the unique sound each produced. His editorial eye was ever active, correcting misspellings or adding a neglected accent—restaurant menus were as vulnerable as students' papers. He never raised his voice in the 25 years I knew him—he preferred to disarm with a well-chosen bon mot or a delicious double entendre. He was a devoted husband and father.

In the significance and eloquence of his contributions to music of our time, Halsey Stevens had few peers. His legacy will continue to be felt as we who knew him go about our lives and our art, deeply grateful for his magnificent and enduring contribution to both.

Ralph Vaughan Williams (1872–1958)

Paul Borg, Professor of Music, Illinois State University, at Normal

Toward the end of a long and productive life, Ralph Vaughan Williams wrote two works for which he has achieved a certain notoriety. The *Romance* for harmonica and orchestra and the *Tuba Concerto* are unusually fine contributions to otherwise neglected repertoires. The challenge of writing a significant composition for such odd solo instruments apparently intrigued Vaughan Williams. Although the *Romance* has not enjoyed wide circulation (for lack of an active concert performer), the *Tuba Concerto* has become a staple of the tuba player's repertoire.

That Vaughan Williams agreed to write the two works is not really surprising, given the distinctive directions his life took. He was born into an upper middle-class family on October 12, 1872 in Down Ampney, Gloucestershire. His grandfather and great grandfather were distinguished lawyers. His father was a priest, and when he died in 1875, the family moved to Leith Hill Place, Surrey to live with the mother's sister. Vaughan Williams's mother was part of the artistic Wedgwood family; Charles Darwin was her uncle.

Vaughan Williams received a traditional British education. Deciding to enter music as a profession, he attended both the Royal Academy of Music and Trinity College, Cambridge, studying with Hubert Parry, Charles Wood, and Charles Villiers Stanford. Vaughan Williams was not generally viewed as an especially promising musician. Yet, his persistence and high degree of self-motivation and self-criticism allowed him to become the most individual and distinguished composer of his generation. His formal education lasted well into his thirties and included the then-requisite travel to Germany

(Berlin, to study with Max Bruch) and then to France (Paris, to study with Ravel, who was three years younger than Vaughan Williams).

Several interesting facets of his character influenced the course of his career. His keen sense of the nature of friendship and his constant striving for excellence led him to a constructive relationship with Gustav Holst. They corresponded regularly, and each submitted new compositions to the other for criticism—even when, later in their careers, the two were quite distant in musical style and inclinations.

His sense of civic duty led him on the one hand to organize the Leith Hill festival, which he ran from 1905 to 1955. Only with increasing age did he gradually relinquish the organizational and musical duties associated with it. On the other hand, that civic sense led him at age 42 to volunteer in Great Britain's World War I efforts. He served as an orderly in the Royal Army Medical Corps in England, France, and Greece. Later, he was put in charge of organizing amateur musical events involving the troops. During World War II, he turned his hand to helping refugees, organizing concerts, and, for the first time, composing film music.

Of great importance to his musical development was his interest in English music—church music, Elizabethan and Jacobean music, and folk songs. Like several other composers of the early twentieth century (Bartók, Kodály, Grainger) Vaughan Williams avidly collected folk songs from different areas of his country. He also accepted the task of selecting and editing the tunes of *The English Hymnal* of 1906. These activities aided his personal attempts to find for himself a distinct, yet English, musical identity. Beginning in the first decade of the century, his compositions exhibit both qualities.

Vaughan Williams's output reflects his own varying interests and creative opportunities while maintaining his personal voice. Throughout his career he wrote wonderful vocal music. The *Songs of Travel* (1901); *On Wenlock Edge* (1908–1909) for voice, piano, and string quartet; and the *Ten Blake Songs* (1957), for voice and oboe, demonstrate his sensitive ear for novel colors in creating appropriate, interesting settings of outstanding texts. Supporting his efforts in encouraging amateur music making are his many settings of folk songs for solo voice and for chorus in varying vocal dispositions. Large-scale works involving voices with orchestra range from the *Sea Symphony* (No. 1, 1903–1909) and the oratorio *Sancta civitas* (1923–25) to the popular *Serenade to Music* (1938) and his Christmas cantata, *Hodie* (1953–54). Vaughan Williams also made effective use of a "wordless" chorus, as in *Flos campi* (1925), for solo viola, small orchestra, and chorus.

His stage works share the same general neglect that similar English repertoire, save that of Britten, suffers. Though few in number, these works demonstrate the powerful, dramatic effect his musical idiom achieves. Examples include the masque for dancing, *Job* (1927–30); the ballad opera, *Hugh the Drover* (1910–14); the extraordinary *Riders to the Sea* (1937); and the morality play, *The Pilgrim's Progress* (completed in 1951).

Vaughan Williams is most frequently heard in compositions for instrumental ensembles. He contributed important works for wind (or military) band, such as the *English Folk Song Suite* (1923) and *Toccata marziale* (1924). His symphonies—nine of them—reach from early in his career to the very end of his life. Like comparable works by Sibelius or Nielsen, they define an evolution in the concept of what symphonic works may be. The variety of moods and sounds and the innovative treatments of the symphonic form place them at the summit of his musical achievement.

As individual as the composer are the works for solo instrument and orchestra. That Vaughan Williams wrote for viola, oboe, harmonica, and tuba is a measure of his lack of concern with what tradition dictates and his delight in taking on challenges and filling requests.

It cannot be said that Vaughan Williams single-handedly resurrected England, "Das Land ohne Musik," from the musical poverty associated with the nation's composers during the eighteenth and nineteenth centuries. His is, however, probably the most individual voice among English composers of the first half of the twentieth century.

Alec Wilder—A Short Biography (1907–1980)

Gunther Schuller, Loonis McGlohon, and Robert Levy

Alec Wilder's music is a unique blend of American musical traditions—among them jazz and the American popular song—and basic Classical European forms and techniques. As such, it fiercely resists all labeling. Although it often pained Alec that his music was not more widely accepted by either jazz or Classical performers, he was undeterred and wrote a great deal of music of remarkable originality in many forms: sonatas, suites, concertos, operas, ballets, art songs, woodwind quintets, brass quintets, jazz suites, and hundreds of popular songs.

Many times his music wasn't jazzy enough for the "jazz-ers," or "highbrow," "Classical," or "avant-garde" enough for the Classical establishment. In essence, Wilder's music was so unusual in its originality that it did not fit in any of the pre-ordained musical slots and stylistic pigeonholes. His music was never out of vogue because, in effect, it was never in vogue, its nonstereotypical specialness virtually precluding any widespread acceptance.

In his book *Alec Wilder and His Friends*, Whitney Balliett dubbed Wilder "The President of the Derrière-garde," and to many Classical critics he was a "conservative craftsman," "lacking in innovation," and not to be taken very seriously. Irving Kolodin, a champion of Wilder's music, commended his native urban style, lamenting that it never became "politically fashionable," as did the music of many of his contemporaries.

Wilder, at his best, represents a fascinating amalgam of three quite different composer-archetypes all rolled into one: Gershwin, Poulenc, and Villa-Lobos. In its baldest outlines, Wilder's oeuvre is unusually diverse and characteristically American, a synthesis of the brilliant song writer (Gershwin);

the not-too-intellectual, traditional, and determinedly conservative composer of easily accessible American-style *Gebrauchsmusik*, making use of popular and jazz elements as a matter of course (Poulenc); and a sometimes uncritical, too-casual writer who writes too much too easily—like Shakespeare's old bromide about loving too well but not wisely (Villa-Lobos). Alec Wilder was born Alexander Lafayette Chew Wilder, in Rochester, New York, on February 16, 1907. He studied briefly at the Eastman School of Music, but as a composer he was largely self-taught. As a young man he moved to New York City and made the Algonquin Hotel—that remarkable enclave of American literati and artistic intelligentsia—his permanent home, although he traveled widely and often.

Mitch Miller and Frank Sinatra were initially responsible for getting Wilder's music to the public. Beginning in 1939, Miller organized recordings of Wilder's octets. Combining elements of Classical chamber music, popular melodies, and a jazz rhythm section, the octets became popular—and eventually legendary—through these recordings. Wilder wrote over twenty octets, giving them whimsical titles, such as *Neurotic Goldfish*, *The Amorous Poltergeist*, and *Sea Fugue, Mama*.

In 1945, Frank Sinatra, an early fan of Wilder's music and an avid supporter, persuaded Columbia Records to record some of Wilder's solo wind works with string orchestra, with Sinatra conducting. The two men became lifelong friends, and Sinatra recorded many of Wilder's popular songs. His last song, *A Long Night*, was written in response to a 1980 request from Sinatra for a "saloon" song.

It is a relative rarity for a composer to enjoy a close relationship with Classical musicians, jazz musicians, and popular singers. Wilder was such a composer, endearing himself to a relatively small but very loyal coterie of performers, and successfully appealing to their diverse styles and conceptions. He wrote art songs for distinguished sopranos Jan DeGaetani and Eileen Farrell, chamber music for the New York Woodwind and New York Brass quintets, and large instrumental works for conductors Erich Leinsdorf, Frederick Fennell, Gunther Schuller, Sarah Caldwell, David Zinman, Donald Hunsberger, and Frank Battisti, many of whom premiered his works for orchestra or wind ensemble. Concert soloists who recorded or premiered his music include John Barrows, horn; Bernard Garfield, bassoon; Harvey Phillips, tuba; David Soyer, cello; Gary Karr, string bass; Barry Snyder, piano; Samuel Baron, James Pellerite, and Virginia Nanzetta, flute; Donald Sinta, saxophone; Robert Levy, trumpet; and Gordon Stout, marimba. John Barrows served as friend and mentor to Wilder, not only urging him to compose in the larger forms but also introducing him to many of his musician colleagues.

Jazz musicians fascinated Wilder with their gift for creating extemporaneous compositions. Among those for whom he composed major works were Marian McPartland, piano; Stan Getz, Zoot Sims, and Gerry Mulligan, saxophone; and Doc Severinsen and Clark Terry, trumpet. Entire albums of his songs and shorter pieces were recorded by Bob Brookmeyer, trombone; and Roland Hanna and Marian McPartland, piano. Individual Wilder songs have been recorded, notably by Cab Calloway, Red Norvo, Keith Jarrett, Don Menza, Jimmy Rowles, and Kenny Burrell.

Despite the sinuous angular melodies and unorthodox forms of his songs, Wilder was admired and respected not only by Frank Sinatra and Cab Calloway, but by Mabel Mercer, Jackie and Roy Kral, Mildred Bailey, Peggy Lee, Tony Bennett, and, more recently, Marlene VerPlank and Barbara Lea. For Mabel Mercer (whom Wilder called the Guardian of Songs), he wrote many of his finest popular as well as art songs. She responded by making definitive recordings of a number of them. Among the best-known songs are *It's So Peaceful in the Country* (written for Mildred Bailey), *I'll Be Around, While We're Young,* and *Blackberry Winter.* Sometimes Wilder wrote the lyrics for his songs, but more often he collaborated with such outstanding lyricists as William Engvick, Johnny Mercer, Arnold Sundgaard, and Loonis McGlohon.

Wilder's interest in children brought about hundreds of piano pieces, easy study pieces for many different instruments, the well-known *A Children's Introduction to the Orchestra,* and the song book *Lullabies and Night Songs,* illustrated by Maurice Sendak. His cantata, *Children's Pleas for Peace,* is a testament to his hopes for a better world for young people. He also wrote many children's songs for television productions and records, such as *The Churkendoose*, which was performed by Ray Bolger, and a version of *Pinocchio* starring Mickey Rooney. Additionally, the children of musician friends were remembered with many solo chamber works.

In the early 1950s Wilder became increasingly drawn to writing concert music for soloists, chamber ensembles, and orchestras. He produced dozens of compositions for the concert hall, writing in his typically melodious and ingratiating style. His works are fresh, strong, lyrical, and very much in the American grain. Many pieces include movements that express a kind of melancholy desolation, an unself-pitying loneliness, in contrast to the more buoyant and witty surrounding fast movements.

Alec Wilder wrote music because he said it was the only thing that could content his spirit. He declared, "I didn't do well in terms of financial reward or recognition. But that was never the point." He shunned publicity and was uncomfortable with celebrity. If he never was one to get grants, receive commissions, or win prizes, it is because he never sought such favors. A deep distrust of institutions, combined with an extraordinary shyness verging on an inferiority complex, prevented him from circulating and operating in the composers' world in the ways generally expected of composers. Nonetheless, his awards eventually—late in life—included an honorary doctorate from the Eastman School of Music, the Peabody Award, an unused Guggenheim Fellowship just before his death, an Avon Foundation grant, the Deems Taylor ASCAP Award, and a National Book Award nomination—all of them having to do with *American Popular Song: The Great Innovators, 1900–1950*, (written with James T. Maher), which is undoubtedly the definitive work on the subject. Wilder included almost everyone who had written a song of quality, but said not one word about himself or any of the hundreds—maybe thousands—of pieces he wrote.

No one will ever be sure just how much music Wilder wrote. Sketches of music—sometimes entire pieces—were written on small scraps of manuscript paper while he rode a train, sat on a park bench, or waited in an airport. Scattered about in private collections of Wilder's friends are dozens of compositions which never reached performance or publication. Some may still lie in piano benches and desk drawers wherever Wilder visited, for he wrote almost entirely for friends, and most of his pieces were gifts to them or their children.

What those who knew him well respected in Alec Wilder was his absolute independence and incorruptible aesthetic integrity. For years Alec wrote music of taste and quality with that personal melodic touch that was all his own, unaffected by musical fashion or fads, and never accepting any form of financial remuneration. And no one was more devoted to the musician in providing a playable, functional literature for all those instruments and instrumental ensembles which most composers generally ignore. It was almost a mission in Alec's life to assuage the thirst for good music for the so-called underdog instruments: bass, tuba, euphonium, horn, marimba. Alec was truly the musicians' friend—an American original.

Despite his slightly rumpled-professor look, Alec Wilder always had a touch of elegance and style, always wearing coat and tie, reflecting a comparable blend of spontaneous looseness and formal discipline in his music. There is also humor—sly humor, the humor of an intelligent, sensitive mind—in his music. Wilder was generous to a fault, famous for bringing his friends presents of books. He was also unpredictable, as is his music. Just when one seems to have guessed where he will take us in the next phrase, he surprises us by taking a completely unlikely turn—which in retrospect almost always seems inevitable and right. Not all of Wilder's compositions are light and happy and easily accessible: some of his music—especially that written in his last years—is dark and anguished, reflecting a deep loneliness. And there were sometimes prolonged periods of discouragement and cultural isolation during which Alec found it impossible to write music at all.

Although he protested the label (perhaps sometimes too vigorously), Alec Wilder was a bona fide eccentric. If some of his music sometimes has a lopsided, irregular shape, it is because he intended to throw us off guard in making a musical or emotional point. In his popular songs he often created seven- and nine-bar phrases which feel as natural as the more orthodox eight-bar structures of Tin Pan Alley. That he could also work well within these more-traditional forms is borne out by hundreds of songs and instrumental pieces. Alongside his more complex sinuous melodies, Wilder could also create tunes of haunting simplicity. *I'll Be Around* is surely an extraordinary example of the latter, while the ravishing theme of "Serenade" (from the *Jazz Suite for Four Horns*) is a superior representative of the former, a melody worthy of an Ellington or a Gershwin, or a Schubert, and arguably one of the most beautiful melodies ever composed in our century.

Wilder died of lung cancer on Christmas Eve, 1980 in Gainesville, Florida—"just in time to keep from becoming better known," as he might have joked. The successful National Public Radio 56-show series "American Popular Song," which he hosted with Loonis McGlohon (his co-author in later years), was bringing about a renaissance of popular song. People were beginning to seek interviews with Wilder, and this attention made him nervous. Had he lived, he probably would not have had enough courage to attend either the 1983 ceremony at which he was inducted into the Songwriter's Hall of Fame or the 1989 dedication of the Alec Wilder Reading Room in the Sibley Music Library at the Eastman School of Music.

Once, when his guard was down, Wilder wrote the following poem, which, was read by Thomas M. Hampson at Wilder's funeral service. All the attributes mentioned live on in the music of Alec Wilder.

> Beauty! Art! Wit!
> Wonderment! Humility!
> Arrogance! Style!
> Virtue! Decency!
> Patience!
> And all the others,
> Gone, trampled by the
> Newly-polished jack boots
> Of the clog-suited society.
> I am a stranger here, from
> Another planet;
> Not spotted yet, but
> Getting peculiar stares.

Forbidden entrance to
All the places where
Air remains,
Where green is true
and water unmolested.

In any other time,
(Excepting Attila's)
I'd be a hero
Why, they'd even name
An alley after me
And put a blotting-paper
Plaque on all my doors
Not because I was great
But because I insisted on
All the words and ways rejected by
Those who wait ferally
In the ancient trees.

GARY BIRD is Professor of Music at Indiana University of Pennsylvania, where he teaches Tuba and Euphonium, Introduction to Music, Jazz Ensemble, and Jazz Perspectives. He has been a member of the Fort Worth Symphony Orchestra and is presently Principal Tubist of the Johnstown and Westmoreland symphonies.